Study Guide
to Accompany

ANTHROPOLOGY
A Perspective on the Human Condition

Margaret Rauch
Co-Director, Academic Learning Center
St. Cloud State University

Robert H. Lavenda
St. Cloud State University

Mayfield Publishing Company
Mountain View, California
London • Toronto

International Standard Book Number: 1-55934-402-4

Manufactured in the United States of America
10 9 8 7 6 5 4 3 2 1

Mayfield Publishing Company
1280 Villa Street
Mountain View, California 94041

Contents

Find It Fast!

Study Strategies

Here's where to find the Study Strategy you need when you need it:

If you need some advice on: Turn to Chapter(s):

Introduction: To the Student

Study strategies are included within this *Study Guide* to help you learn the information in *Anthropology: A Perspective on the Human Condition* and prepare for your tests in the course. Jenkins' model of learning and remembering (cited in Bransford, 1979) was used as a guide for the strategies. Based upon this model, you should ask yourself the following questions:

1. What is the extent of my background knowledge in anthropology?
2. What new information will I have to learn? How difficult is the information?
3. What will I have to do to learn the information? That is, what strategies will help me?
4. What type of tests will I have to take?

One of the keys to being a successful student is to become an independent learner. Thinking about the answers to the questions above is an important step in this process. Another step is to know how and when to use different strategies which will help you learn and remember information (Brown & Palincsar, 1982). In addition, the affective component (McCombs & Whistler, 1989) is important because you have to be motivated to try different strategies and incorporate the strategies into your study method.

In summary, the purpose of incorporating study strategies into this *Study Guide* is to help you become more aware of the way you learn and remember information, and to encourage you to add new strategies to your study method. The order of the *Study Skill* segments works well in preparing students for this course, but it is certainly not the only way to use the segments. If you need help right away on a topic that's not covered until later in the *Study Guide*, don't wait! The principles in the segments, although sometimes illustrated by material from a specific chapter, apply everywhere. Remember, this *Study Guide* is designed to benefit *you!*

This *Study Guide* was also designed to help you by giving you a chance to review the key terms in the text and to get accustomed to the kinds of multiple choice exam questions you might encounter in this course.

Finally, each chapter has a section called Arguing Anthropology. These are not designed to be questions only for students considering an anthropology major. They're written to be provocative, to be argued, and to stimulate you to make anthropology something that has a connection with your life and our collective lives on this planet. Our hope is that many students will form study groups—one of the most effective ways to learn material of any kind—and will find these questions worth discussing, almost as a relief from the more focused work on the course.

Remember, no one is born an anthropologist. Your instructor and the authors of your textbook began as you are beginning: sitting in an introductory class. They found the material and the approach really exciting intellectually, and they made the decision to continue in anthropology. Our hope is that you too will find that excitement. Good luck!

Chapter 1: The Anthropological Perspective

STUDY STRATEGY: **PREVIEW/READ/REVIEW METHOD OF READING**

Students often ask for study tips to improve their comprehension and retention of information so they can do better on their tests. Within this Study Guide, ideas for reading and studying *Cultural Anthropology: A Perspective on the Human Condition* will be discussed.

Getting Started

Previewing this anthropology textbook is a good way to become familiar with the structure and content of the book. First, read the Preface to learn why the book was written. Second, preview the table of contents to learn how the content in the book is structured. Do you have problems remembering what you read, concentrating on the information? Is much of the information new to you? Do you think this anthropology course will be a real challenge? If so, try the Preview/Read/Review method of reading.

Previewing Chapter 1

Previewing a chapter provides you with the focus, the purpose, of the whole chapter. Complete the following three steps when previewing Chapter 1.

1. Go to the table of contents, note the title of Chapter 1, The Anthropological Perspective, and read the outline of main headings:

   What Is Anthropology?
   The Concept of Culture
   The Cross-Disciplinary Discipline
       Physical Anthropology (Biological Anthropology)
       Cultural Anthropology
       Anthropological Linguistics
       Archaeology
       Applied Anthropology
   Anthropology, Science, and Storytelling
   Some Key Scientific Concepts
       Assumptions
       Evidence
       Hypotheses
       Testability
       Theories
       Objectivity
   Uses of Anthropology
   Key Terms
   Chapter Summary
   Suggested Readings

2. This outline of Chapter 1 provides you with the structure of the content. Leaf through the chapter. Notice that key vocabulary terms appear in **bold** type and are listed at the end of the chapter.
3. Read the summary. The summary gives you the main concepts and some of the key terms discussed in the chapter.

Reading Chapter 1

Sometimes we find information interesting to read, like the story on pages 1–3. Other times we dread the reading because we think the information is dry and boring, or we are so tired that we experience problems concentrating on the information. Try the following reading approach to overcome these problems and to increase your comprehension and retention.

1. Turn headings into questions. In this chapter, the first heading is already a question: What Is Anthropology? Before beginning to read this section, think about what you know about anthropology. New information can be easier to understand when you use your existing knowledge as a starting point. Read this section, stop, and answer the question: What is anthropology?

2. Ask questions using the new vocabulary. For example, you could ask the following questions for the new vocabulary used in the first section.
   - What makes anthropology holistic?
   - Why is anthropology a comparative discipline?
   - What makes the anthropological perspective evolutionary?
   - What is the difference between biological evolution and cultural evolution?

3. Read the next heading: The Concept of Culture. Think about what you already know about culture. Then ask: What is involved in culture? and, Is what I know about culture similar to what anthropologists know? As you read this section, stop and answer your questions. Ask other questions about the vocabulary.

4. Finish the chapter. Go section by section. First, think about what you already know. Then, turn each heading into a question, read the section, stop at the end of the section, and answer your question. Develop more questions over the section.

Reviewing Chapter 1

Are you usually thrilled and delighted to finish a chapter? Do you usually close the book and begin another project? To ensure that you understand the information and to help yourself remember the information, try the following strategies.

1. If you underlined or took notes while you read, review what you underlined or wrote. Recite the ideas.

2. Sometimes a major section of the chapter is divided into parts; for example, The Cross-Disciplinary Discipline is divided into five parts: Physical Anthropology (Biological Anthropology), Cultural Anthropology, Anthropological Linguistics, Archaeology, and Applied Anthropology. When reviewing and reciting, ask yourself questions: What is the relationship among these five parts? How are the five parts related to The Cross-Disciplinary Discipline? Recognizing the interrelationship between ideas helps you to understand information and to do better on tests.

3. Review the list of key terms. For each one, you could write the page number, definition, and an example right in the book.

4. Another method of studying vocabulary is to make vocabulary cards. Use notecards, writing the term and page number on the front side and the meaning plus an example on the back side. Review the cards until you can recite the information without having to look at the answer. Take the cards with you to review during the day. For example, do you ever have to wait in line? Have five minutes before a teacher starts class? Are you waiting for a friend at the library? Use this "wait" time to review a few cards. You can also divide the cards into "known" and "unknown" piles. Study with a friend and quiz each other on the vocabulary. Do the Key Terms Review in this Study Guide.

5. Do the questions in this Study Guide. If you answered a question incorrectly, analyze why you got it wrong. Did you just forget? Did you mix up several key terms? Was the question a fact or an application question? Application questions are usually more difficult because they require you to apply information to a new situation.

EXERCISES

Key Terms Review

Use the appropriate key term(s) in each sentence that follows.

anthropological linguistics
anthropology
applied anthropology
archaeology
assumptions
biocultural
comparative
cultural anthropology
culture

ethnography
ethnology
evidence
evolutionary
fieldwork
holism
hypotheses
informants
language

myths
objectivity
paleoanthropologists
physical anthropology
 (biological anthropology)
primatologists
race
scientific theories
testability

1. _____ is the study of human nature, human society, and the human past.

2. That part of the anthropological perspective that tries to integrate all that is known about human beings and their activities, at the highest and most inclusive level, is known as _____.

3. Seeking evidence for generalizations from any and all human societies, anywhere in the world, and any and all periods of human history, including those periods dating from the emergence of _____ is the study of human nature, human society, and the human past.

2. That part of the anthropological perspective that tries to integrate all that is known about human beings and their activities, at the highest and most inclusive level, is known as _____.

3. Seeking evidence for generalizations from any and all human societies, anywhere in the world, and any and all periods of human history, including those periods dating from the emergence of human-like primates some five million years ago, makes the anthropological perspective _____.

4. To call anthropology _____ is to recognize the characteristic of the anthropological perspective that requires anthropologists to place their observations about human nature, human society, or the human past in a temporal framework that pays attention to change over time.

5. _____ consists of sets of learned behavior and ideas that human beings acquire as members of society, used both to adapt to and to transform the wider world in which we live.

6. To say that anthropology is _____ is to pay attention to the interconnections of both our genetically guided biological makeup, including our brain, nervous system, and anatomy, and the learned cultural traditions that help us find food, shelter, and mates, and teach us how to rear our young.

7. The subfield of anthropology in which anthropologists look at human beings as biological organisms, trying to discover both what makes human beings different from other living organisms and what human beings share with other members of the animal kingdom, is known as _____.

8. _____ is the term used to refer to a social grouping based on perceived physical differences and cloaked in the language of biology.

9. Scholars who specialize in the study of the closest living relatives of human beings are called _____.

10. _____ are scholars who search the earth for the fossilized bones and teeth of our earliest ancestors.

11. The subfield of anthropology that shows how variation in the beliefs and behaviors of members of different human groups is shaped by sets of learned behavior and ideas that human beings acquire as members of society is known as _____.

12. _____ is the symbolic system we use to encode our experience of the world and of each other.

13. _____ is the branch of anthropology concerned with the study of human languages.

14. _____ is an extended period of close involvement with the people in whose language or way of life anthropologists are interested.

15. Those people in a particular culture who work with anthropologists and provide them with insights about their way of life are called _____.

16. _____ is an anthropologist's description of a particular culture, while _____ is the comparative study of many cultures.

17. _____ is a kind of cultural anthropology of the human past, involving the analysis of material remains left behind by earlier human societies.

18. A subfield of anthropology in which information gathered from the other subfields is used to solve practical cross-cultural problems is called _____.

19. _____ are stories whose truth seems self-evident, because these stories do such a good job of integrating our personal experiences with a wider set of assumptions about the way society, or the world in general, must operate.

20. _____ are the basic understandings about the way the world works that people never question, while _____ is what we can see when we examine a particular part of the world with great care.

21. Statements that assert a particular connection between fact and interpretation, such as "The bones found at the Hadar site in Ethiopia belonged to an extinct form of primate that appears ancestral to modern human beings," are known as _____.

22. _____ refers to the capacity of scientific hypotheses to be matched against nature in order to check whether the hypotheses are confirmed or refuted.

23. A coherent series of testable hypotheses deployed to explain a body of material evidence is known as a _____.

24. The separation of observation and reporting from the researcher's wishes may be referred to as _____.

Multiple Choice Questions

1. "Integrating what is known about human beings and their activities at an inclusive level" is a definition of _____.
   a. holism
   b. comparison
   c. evolution
   d. culture

2. A person visits another country and returns with stories about how primitive and backward the people are. This would appear to be an example of _____.
   a. a comparative approach
   b. holism
   c. ethnocentrism
   d. cultural relativism

3. When anthropologists talk about "Culture with a capital C," they are referring to _____.
   a. the fine arts of any group of human beings
   b. a fundamental attribute of human beings
   c. specific traditions of learned behavior
   d. the innate instincts of human beings

4. The study of human beings as biological organisms is known as _____.
   a. archaeology
   b. paleoanatomy
   c. paleoanthropology
   d. physical anthropology

5. An anthropologist has been hired to research why a specific group of people in the South American Andes do not send their children to school, and to suggest strategies for encouraging them to do so. This anthropologist is most likely engaged in _____.
   a. cultural anthropology
   b. applied anthropology
   c. physical anthropology
   d. linguistic anthropology

6. Cultural anthropologists live with the people they are studying during an extended period called _____.
   a. fact collecting
   b. fieldwork
   c. interviewing
   d. anthropological research

7. When cultural anthropologists both get involved in social activities and watch social activities, they are involved in a research methodology called _____.
   a. fitting in
   b. interviewing
   c. participant-observation
   d. case study

8. One of the potentials of anthropology is to help people _____.
   a. learn to cope with cultural differences
   b. develop a more nuanced approach to cultural diversity
   c. dispel harmful stereotypes of others
   d. all of the above

Arguing Anthropology

Questions for discussion and thought:

1. Why is comparison so important in anthropology?

2. Why might human diversity be threatening in some circumstances?

ANSWER KEY

Key Terms Review

1. Anthropology
2. holism
3. comparative
4. evolutionary
5. Culture
6. biocultural
7. physical anthropology *or* biological anthropology
8. Race
9. primatologists
10. Paleoanthropologists
11. cultural anthropology
12. Language
13. Anthropological linguistics
14. Fieldwork
15. informants
16. Ethnography, ethnology
17. Archaeology
18. applied anthropology
19. Myths
20. Assumptions, evidence
21. hypotheses
22. Testability
23. scientific theory
24. objectivity

Multiple Choice Questions

1. a
2. c
3. b
4. d
5. b
6. b
7. c
8. d

Chapter 2: Evolution

STUDY STRATEGY: READING YOUR TEXTBOOK

Previewing Chapter 2

Preview Chapter 2, Evolution, to learn the structure (outline) of information. Also, look at the pictures and graphs. Do you have some prior knowledge of any of this information? Prior knowledge can make learning and remembering easier.

Outline of Chapter 2:

Evolutionary Theory
Material Evidence for Evolution
Pre-Darwinian Views of the Natural World
    Essentialism
    The Great Chain of Being
    Natural Theology: Catastrophism and Uniformitarianism
    Transformational Evolution
The Theory of Natural Selection
Unlocking the Secrets of Heredity
    Mendel
    "There Is No 'Race Memory' in Biology, Only in Books"
Genotype, Phenotype, and the Norm of Reaction
What Does Evolution Mean?
Key Terms
Chapter Summary

Reading Chapter 2

Reading the assigned chapters before going to class will help you understand the lecture better and will make note-taking easier. Before you read each section, think about what you already know. For example, before beginning to read the section Science and Evolution, ask yourself: What do I know about science? What do I know about evolution? Remember, your background knowledge may be helpful when you learn new information. As you read, ask questions (Is this what I know? What new ideas are the authors telling me about science and evolution?), read the section, stop, and answer your questions. It really does not take much time to stop and answer your questions, and this added step is effective as preparation for tests.

Continue turning the headings into questions, thinking about what you already know, then reading, and reciting your answers. Underline, highlight, or take notes as you read.

Reviewing

Go back and review your notes or what you underlined. For the vocabulary you did not know, decide to either write the page number, meaning, and an example in your textbook, or to use notecards. Write the word on the front of the card, and the meaning and an example on the back of the card.

EXERCISES

Key Terms Review

Use the appropriate key term(s) in each sentence that follows.

alleles
catastrophism
chromosomes
common descent
continuous variation
crossing over
discontinuous variation
DNA (deoxyribonucleic acid)
essentialism
evolution
evolutionary theory
fitness
gene
genetics

genotype
genus
Great Chain of Being
heterozygous
homozygous
linkage
locus
meiosis
Mendelian inheritance
mitosis
mutation
natural selection
norm of reaction

pangenesis
phenotype
pleiotropy
polygeny
principle of independent
   assortment
principle of segregation
species
taxonomy
transformational evolution
uniformitarianism
variational evolution

1. The set of testable hypotheses that assert that living organisms can change over time and give rise to new kinds of living organisms, so that all organisms ultimately can be said to share a common ancestry is known as _____.

2. _____ is the process of change over time.

3. Derived from Plato, _____ is the belief in fixed ideas, or forms, that exist perfect and unchanging in eternity.

4. A comprehensive framework for interpreting the world, based on Aristotelian principles and elaborated during the Middle Ages, in which every kind of living organism was linked to every other kind by the least possible degree of difference was called _____.

5. A _____ is a classification; in biology, it is the classification of various kinds of organisms.

6. A reproductive community of populations (reproductively isolated from others) that occupies a specific niche in nature is a _____.

7. A _____ is the level of a Linnaean taxonomy in which different species are grouped together on the basis of their similarities to one another.

8. The notion that natural disasters, such as floods, are responsible for the extinction of species, which are then replaced by new species, is known as _____.

9. _____ is the notion that an understanding of current processes can be used to reconstruct the past history of the earth, based on the assumption that the same gradual processes of erosion and uplift that change the earth's surface today had also been at work in the past.

10. Also called Lamarckian evolution, _____ assumes essentialist species and a uniformly changing environment. Each individual member of a species transforms itself to meet the challenges of a changed environment through the laws of use and disuse and the inheritance of acquired characters.

11. Darwin's claim that similar living species must all have shared an ancestor is known as _____.

12. _____ is a two-step, mechanistic explanation of how descent with modification takes place: (1) variation is generated, ultimately through mutation, and (2) those variants best suited to the current environment survive and produce more offspring than other variants.

13. The Darwinian theory of evolution is called _____; it assumes that variant members of a species respond differently to environmental challenges: those variants that are more successful (fitter) survive and produce more offspring, who inherit the variants that made their parents fit.

14. _____ is a measure of an organism's ability to compete in the struggle for existence: those individuals whose variant traits better equip them to compete with other members of their species for limited resources are more likely to survive and reproduce than those individuals who lack such traits.

15. A theory of heredity, now discredited, suggesting that an organism's physical traits are passed on from one generation to the next in the form of multiple distinct particles given off by all parts of an organism, different proportions of which get passed on to offspring via sperm or egg, is called _____.

16. Non-blending, single-particle genetic inheritance is called _____.

17. The _____ is the principle of Mendelian inheritance which states that an individual gets one gene for each trait (i.e. one half of the required pair) from each parent.

18. The _____ is the principle of Mendelian inheritance which states that each pair of genes separates independently of every other pair when germ cells (egg and sperm) are formed.

19. The scientific study of biological heredity is called _____.

20. A fertilized egg that has received the same allele from each parent for a particular trait is said to be

_____.

21. A fertilized egg that has received a different allele from each parent for the same trait is said to be

_____.

22. _____ refers to that section of the DNA molecule carrying genetic information

for a particular phenotypic trait.

23. The different forms that a given gene might take are called _____.

24. _____ are sets of paired bodies in the nucleus of cells, made of DNA and

containing the hereditary genetic information that organisms pass on to their offspring.

25. During the process of _____ the chromosomes in the nucleus of the cell

duplicate and line up along the center of the cell. The cell then divides, each daughter cell taking one

full set of paired chromosomes with it.

26. The process of _____ begins with chromosome duplication and the formation

of two daughter cells; however, each daughter cell then divides again without chromosome duplication

and, as a result, contains only a single set of chromosomes.

27. _____ is an inheritance pattern in which unrelated phenotypic traits regularly

occur together and never occur independently of one another.

28. The phenomenon of _____ occurs when part of one chromosome breaks off

and reattaches itself to a different chromosome during meiosis (also called *incomplete* linkage).

29. _____ is a pattern of phenotypic variation in which the phenotype (for example,

flower color) exhibits sharp breaks from one member of the population to the next.

30. The term used to refer to the way in which many genes are responsible for producing a single phenotypic

trait, such as skin color, is _____.

31. _____ is a pattern of variation in which the phenotypic traits (height, hair

color, and so on) grade imperceptibly from one member of the population to another, without sharp

breaks.

32. The phenomenon whereby a single gene may affect more than one phenotypic trait is known as

_____.

33. _____ is the creation of a new allele for a gene when the portion of the DNA

molecule to which it corresponds is suddenly altered.

34. The structure that carries the genetic heritage of an organism as a kind of blueprint for the organism's construction and development is known as _____.

35. A particular position on the DNA strand where specific genetic information is found is called a gene's

_____.

36. The _____ is the information about particular biological traits that are encoded in DNA.

37. The observable, measurable overt characteristics of an organism: _____

38. _____ is a table or graph that displays the possible range of phenotypic outcomes for a given genotype in different environments.

Multiple Choice Questions

1. Material evidence of evolutionary change can be found in _____.
   a. the pattern of distribution of living species
   b. the chemical makeup of limestone deposits
   c. the fossil record
   d. both a and c

2. The theory associated with Georges Cuvier that holds that over time some species were wiped out and replaced by others is called _____.
   a. catastrophism
   b. the Great Chain of Being
   c. natural selection
   d. uniformitarianism

3. The term "variational evolution" is associated with which of the following scholars?
   a. Georges Cuvier
   b. Charles Darwin
   c. Lamarck
   d. Charles Lyell

4. Which of the following is NOT a principle of Darwin's theory of evolution by natural selection?
   a. heredity
   b. natural selection
   c. linkage
   d. variation

5. In Darwinian terms, who are the fit?
   a. the strongest
   b. those who live the longest
   c. those who leave behind offspring
   d. those who cooperate with others

6. When peas with red flowers are crossed with peas with white flowers, what will be the ratio of one trait to the other in the second generation?
    a. 1:1
    b. 2:1
    c. 3:1
    d. 4:1

7. A fertilized egg that has received the same form of a specific gene from each parent is called
_____.
    a. homozygous
    b. heterozygous
    c. allele-identical
    d. chromosomal

8. The allele that causes the feathers of a chicken to be white also works to slow down the chicken's body growth. This is an example of _____.
    a. mutation
    b. linkage
    c. pleiotropy
    d. polygeny

9. The theory of "race memory" is based on the idea that _____.
    a. genetic inheritance is unchanging inheritance
    b. lived experiences can become part of the genetic inheritance of a group
    c. the present state of a species is a consequence of its history
    d. the phenotype is a result of the genotype

10. The relationship between genotype and phenotype is always _____.
    a. direct
    b. mediated by the environment
    c. predictable
    d. transformed through mutation

Arguing Anthropology

Questions for discussion and thought:

1. Even though the Darwinian concept of natural selection does not require the idea of "the survival of the fittest," why is the idea so popular?

2. Consider the following statement: "The only certainty about the future of our species is that it is limited. Of all the species that have ever existed 99.999% are extinct." What might be the implications for human beings and for human societies?

ANSWER KEY

Key Terms Review

1. evolutionary theory
2. Evolution
3. essentialism
4. Great Chain of Being
5. taxonomy
6. species
7. genus
8. catastrophism
9. Uniformitarianism
10. transformational evolution
11. common descent
12. Natural selection
13. variational evolution
14. Fitness
15. pangenesis
16. Mendelian inheritance
17. principle of segregation
18. principle of independent assortment
19. genetics
20. homozygous
21. heterozygous
22. Gene
23. alleles
24. Chromosomes
25. mitosis
26. meiosis
27. Linkage
28. crossing over
29. Discontinuous variation
30. polygeny
31. Continuous variation
32. pleiotropy
33. Mutation
34. DNA (deoxyribonucleic acid)
35. locus
36. genotype
37. phenotype
38. Norm of reaction

Multiple Choice Questions

1. d
2. a
3. b
4. c
5. c
6. c
7. a
8. c
9. b
10. b

Chapter 3: Microevolution and Macroevolution: Human Evolution in the Short and Long Term

STUDY STRATEGY: FACT AND APPLICATION TEST QUESTIONS

Two types of questions commonly found on tests are fact and application questions.

Fact Questions

Fact questions can be divided into main idea and detail questions. These questions are usually answered from information easily found in the chapter.

You may remember information covered by main idea questions because of the structure of the chapter. That is, the title of the chapter gives the main topic, the introduction includes the purpose or focus of the chapter, and the headings signal the major and minor topics in the chapter. In addition, the main ideas appear in the summary. The following main idea question was developed from the section The Four Evolutionary Forces:

> Modern evolutionists recognize four evolutionary forces that shape the histories of living organisms. Which one of the following is not one of the evolutionary forces?
> a. natural selection
> b. mutation
> c. developmental acclimatization
> d. gene flow

If you had turned each heading into a question when you read and studied (What are the four evolutionary forces? What is the definition of each force? Example?), and if you had written out vocabulary cards, you would easily recognize that "C" was not one of the four evolutionary forces. This question may be too easy, so let's consider another one:

> Scores from intelligence tests do not prove that racial differences in intelligence are genetically determined. Why?
> a. Racial identity may be determined by skin color, and then it may be assumed that intelligence differs between people of different "races."
> b. There is no universal agreement on the concept of intelligence.
> c. There is no universal agreement that intelligence tests measure "intelligence."
> d. all of the above

When you read the section on intelligence, did you notice that the second paragraph begins with the question, "Do scores on IQ tests prove that racial differences in intelligence are clear-cut and genetically determined?" The above test question is the same question.

Now look at the organization of the second and third paragraphs. The authors pose the question, answer No, and then give three reasons for their answer ("first," "second," "third"), with examples. The answer to the test question is D.

Do IQ scores prove that racial differences in intelligence are clear-cut and genetically determined? They do not. First, the assumption that races are natural kinds assumes that racial boundaries are clear and that traits essential to racial identity (such as skin color) are discrete and nonoverlapping. . . . Second, it is far from clear that there is a single accurately measurable substance, called "intelligence" that some people have more of than others. . . . Third, even if intelligence is such a measurable substance, we don't know that IQ tests actually measure it.

Detail questions can be more difficult because the questions and answers come from information within the paragraphs. For example, the following question might arise from the Sociobiology section.

Sociobiologists believe that the behaviors of all animal societies (e.g. Human beings, ants) _____.

a. have more characteristics that are common than characteristics that are different
b. are different because of the differences in habitat, food, and culture
c. are determined by culture
d. are different because of different evolutionary forces

In answering this question, it would help if you knew the meaning of sociobiology, as well as what sociobiologists believe. The answer is A.

Application Questions

Application questions can be very difficult because they require you not only to know the information but to apply the information to new situations. Students often say, "I knew the information. I memorized the definitions of the terms, and I can recite you anything in my notes." However, "memorizing" usually means students knew the words used in the book for the key terms, and the examples the instructor used in class. This may help a student answer a fact question, but not an application question for which the student had to apply the information to a new situation.

For explanation purposes, let's say there are three levels of information. In Level One you may know the book definition and recognize it on the test. In Level Two you may know the definition and examples used in the book and discussed in class by your teacher. In fact, you may be able to explain the definition and examples in your own words to your classmate, which means you are beginning to understand the concept. In Level Three you read a new situation and know that the new information is another example of the concept you just learned. Now you are beginning to master the concept. You are ready for application questions. Let's discuss an application question from the section Human Variation.

The Olympic Games were held in the high altitudes of Mexico. Runners from the United States who were going to compete in the Olympic Games practiced in the similarly high altitudes of Colorado. This is an example of _____.
a. plasticity
b. founder effect
c. developmental acclimatization
d. inclusive fitness

To answer this question, you must know what the Olympic Games are. You must also know the definition of all the terms. The authors discussed the effect the thin air in the high altitudes of the Andes Mountains in South America has on the lungs: the people living in the high altitudes develop increased lung capacity. If runners from low altitudes are going to compete with runners who are already accustomed to the thin air of the higher altitudes, they must practice in that climate. The answer is "C."

Students are familiar with multiple-choice, true-false, and essay questions. However, many students are unfamiliar and uncomfortable with analogy questions. To solve an analogy question, you have to recognize the relationship between the vocabulary terms, people, events, or things. Let's do some easy analogy questions.

Small is to large as minuscule is to enormous.
Or, Small:Large::Minuscule:Enormous. (Degree of the range of size)

Mother is to daughter as father is to son
Or, Mother:Daughter::Father:Son (Relationship of people)

Harrison Ford is to *The Fugitive* as Tom Cruise is to *The Firm*.
Or, Harrison Ford:*The Fugitive*::Tom Cruise:*The Firm*. (Major movie star and the movie he starred in.)

Now let's discuss the following analogy question from this chapter.

Anagenesis:Cladogenesis::
a. species:individual
b. single species:multiple species
c. gradual change:rapid change
d. movement:equilibrium

Here, if you recall that anagenesis is the slow, gradual transformation of a single species over time, and cladogenesis is the birth of a variety of descendant species from a single ancestral species, the answer will be clear: it is "B." The closest incorrect answer, "C," emphasizes change and gets the anagenesis side of the analogy correct, but there is nothing about the speed of cladogenesis in the text. Answer "A" uses two words that appear in the discussion of anagenesis and cladogenesis, but does not use them in a sensible way. It is possible to argue that movement and equilibrium are related to anagenesis and cladogenesis, but they are reversed.

Test-Taking Analysis

Analyze your test-taking. When you miss questions, what type of question do you miss most often—fact or application questions? Why? Did you read too fast? Skimmed the information? Did you read passively, without asking yourself questions as you read? Did you allow yourself too little time to read, review, and think about the information?

Test-taking problems often occur when students think they know the information and then hit a brick wall when answering questions, especially higher-level questions (application questions) on the test. Because the students did not thoroughly understand the concepts, they could not apply the terms to the new examples used in the test questions and answers. It takes time to learn; so evaluate your background knowledge and decide how much time you need to schedule for your reading and studying and thinking and discussing the information with classmates.

Tips for Studying Your Textbook

In Chapter 1 we discussed the Preview/Read/Review method for reading and studying a chapter. If you are not already using this method, consider using it for your next test. Then compare your comfort level for the two tests. Preread the chapter to gain an understanding of the main ideas which will be discussed in it. Next, turn headings into questions, read, and stop to answer your questions. Finally, organize the information: that is, go back and reread what you underlined or took notes on. Do the questions in this Study Guide to test your knowledge of the information. If you missed any questions, discuss the information with a classmate, your instructor, or a tutor. In addition to the questions offered here, think about other questions your instructor may ask.

Tips for Studying Your Notes

Note-taking will be easier if you read the chapter before attending class. If you do not have time to read the chapter, at least preview it; read the bold headings, graphs, illustrations, and the summary. You will then be able to recognize the main ideas.

Another effective strategy is reviewing your notes often. Reviewing notes as soon as possible after class and reviewing your total set of notes often helps you keep ideas fresh in your memory. You will not need to cram, and you will be able to retrieve the information more easily from your memory when writing the test. Reviewing often can certainly help with fact questions, and these facts can form the foundation for concept building.

Additional note-taking strategies involve cross-checking and discussing your notes with classmates. Have you ever cross-checked your notes and found that your classmates had more information from the lecture than you had? Discussing information with classmates is helpful because you hear the information from another perspective. Other viewpoints can increase your depth of understanding and expand your knowledge of the concept, so you will have a higher comfort level with application questions.

EXERCISES

Key Terms Review

Use the appropriate key term(s) in each sentence that follows.

acclimatization	gene frequencies	mutation
adaptation	gene pool	natural selection
Allen's Rule	genetic drift	parental investment
allometry	group selection	phyletic gradualism
altruism	inclusive fitness	plasticity
anagenesis	indirect bias	population genetics
Bergmann's Rule	kin selection	punctuated equilibrium
cladogenesis	macroevolution	sociobiology
developmental acclimatization	microevolution	species
ethology	mitochondrial DNA	species selection
gene flow		

1. The subfield of evolutionary studies that devotes attention to short-term evolutionary changes that occur within a given species over relatively few generations of geological time is called

    _____.

2. The subfield of evolutionary studies that focuses on long-term evolutionary changes, especially the origins of new species and their diversification across space and over geological time is called

    _____.

3. A _____ is a reproductive community of populations (reproductively isolated from others) that occupies a specific niche in nature.

4. A _____ is made up of all of the genes in the bodies of all members of a given species (or population of a species).

5. _____ refers to the frequency of occurrence of the variants of particular genes (that is, of alleles) within the gene pool.

6. The field that uses statistical analysis to study short-term evolutionary change in large populations is called _____.

7. Genes carried outside the cell nucleus in tiny structures in the cytoplasm are known as _____.

8. _____ is a two-step mechanistic explanation of how descent with modification takes place: (1) variation is generated, ultimately through mutation, and (2) those variants best suited to the current environment survive and produce more offspring than other variants.

9. The creation of a new allele for a gene when the portion of the DNA molecule to which it corresponds is suddenly altered is the process of _____.

10. The exchange of genes that occurs when a given population experiences a sudden expansion due to in-migration of outsiders from another population of the species is known as _____.

11. _____ is defined as random changes in gene frequencies from one generation to the next due to sudden reduction in population size as a result of disaster, disease, or the out-migration of a small subgroup from a larger population.

12. The mutual shaping of organisms and their environments is known as _____.

13. _____ is the physiological flexibility that allows organisms to respond to environmental stresses, such as temperature changes.

14. _____ is change in the way the body functions in response to physical stress; when that stress varies by the length of time an organism lives in a specific environment and the age at which it enters the environment, it is called _____.

15. _____ rule states that (1) animals adapted to cold climates will have larger, more compact bodies to conserve heat and that (2) animals adapted to warm climates will have smaller bodies or long bodies to lose heat.

16. _____ rule states that (1) animals adapted to cold climates should have short, stout limbs in order to conserve heat and that (2) animals adapted to hot climates should have long, slender limbs to lose heat faster.

17. The rate at which different body parts grow in relation to one another is called _____.

18. _____ is defined by its practitioners as the systematic study of the biological basis of all social behavior.

19. The willingness to give up benefits for oneself in order to help someone else is called _____.

20. The sociobiological notion of _____ includes not only the ability of an individual organism to make a living and replace itself but also the similar abilities of all those individuals with whom an organism shares genes.

21. The concept that natural selection will preserve genes for altruistic behaviors if the altruists sacrificed themselves for close kin is called _____.

22. Using an economic metaphor, _____ is the sociobiological explanation for the different patterns of parental involvement in caring for offspring as a consequence of the role of each parent in reproduction.

23. _____ is the study of animal behavior.

24. The pattern of social behavior in which individuals copy several cultural traits at once because these traits are associated with some other factor they find attractive is called _____.

25. When the fitness of individuals depends not only on their own personal characteristics but also on those of the local group to which they belong, the term used is _____.

26. The slow, gradual transformation of a single species over time is known as _____.

27. A theory arguing that one species gradually transforms itself into a new species over time, yet the actual boundary between species can never be detected and can only be drawn arbitrarily, is called _____.

28. The birth of a variety of descendant species from a single ancestral species is called _____.

29. A theory claiming that most of evolutionary history has been characterized by relatively stable species coexisting in an equilibrium that is occasionally punctuated by sudden bursts of speciation, when extinctions are widespread and many new species appear, is known as _____.

30. _____ is the process in which natural selection is seen to operate among variant related species within a single genus, family, or order.

Multiple Choice Questions

1. The study of macroevolution focuses on _____.
   a. large evolutionary changes
   b. long-term evolutionary changes in geologic time
   c. short-term evolutionary changes in ecologic time
   d. evolutionary changes on the individual level

2. From a biological perspective, the ability to interbreed indicates that members of different populations are all members of the same _____.
   a. consanguineal family
   b. interbreeding stock
   c. natural selection category
   d. reproductive community

3. The notion of the so-called Black, Red, Yellow, and White "races" of human beings is based on _____.
   a. biological observation of genetic differences among the different populations
   b. a human need to discriminate
   c. cultural elaboration of a few superficial phenotypic differences
   d. careful observation of behavioral differences

4. In a balanced polymorphism, _____.
   a. the heterozygous genotype is fitter than either of the homozygous genotypes
   b. the homozygous recessive genotype is fitter than either the homozygous dominant or the heterozygous genotype
   c. the homozygous dominant genotype is fitter than either the homozygous recessive or the heterozygous genotype
   d. all three genotypes are equally fit

5. Which of the following body size and shape combinations conserves heat best?
   a. larger and more compact
   b. larger and more linear
   c. smaller and more compact
   d. smaller and more linear

6. Much recent research has demonstrated that IQ scores are _____.
   a. phenotypic traits determined by genes
   b. determined about half by genes and half by the environment
   c. shaped by a range of environmental factors
   d. due to random factors (temperature, noise, etc.) in the test-taking situation

7. The sociobiological explanation for altruism is that _____.
   a. it is a hidden form of self-interest, since the organism only appears to sacrifice itself
   b. organisms sacrifice themselves for close kin who carry many of the same genes
   c. it has never been scientifically established as having occurred in nature
   d. both b and c

8. Daniel is a successful lawyer: smart, well-educated, extremely hard-working, well-dressed; he drives an expensive imported car, and drinks a particular brand of diet cola. Rachel, who wishes to achieve the same success, imitates as much of Daniel's behavior as she can, including drinking the same diet cola; she is contributing to a form of cultural transmission that Boyd and Richerson call _____.
    a. flattery
    b. imitation
    c. indirect bias
    d. group selection

9. Group selection occurs when _____.
    a. the fitness of an individual depends on the behavior of other individuals in a local group
    b. members of a group work together to ensure their survival
    c. passing on genes from one generation to another is no longer significant
    d. individuals behave altruistically

10. anagenesis:cladogenesis::
    a. species:individual
    b. single species:multiple species
    c. gradual change:rapid change
    d. movement:equilibrium

Arguing Anthropology

Questions for discussion and thought:

1. "Physical life and a meaningful life usually, but not always, go together." In your opinion, at what point do they stop going together?

2. As genetic research advances, it becomes increasingly possible for human beings to intervene in the genetic processes that affect them (some examples are the human genome project, assisted reproduction, pre-natal genetic testing, and gene cloning). To what degree *should* human beings intervene in the genetic processes that affect them?

ANSWER KEY

Key Terms Review

1. microevolution
2. macroevolution
3. species
4. gene pool
5. Gene frequencies
6. population genetics
7. mitochondrial DNA
8. Natural selection
9. mutation
10. gene flow
11. Genetic drift
12. adaptation
13. Plasticity
14. Acclimatization; developmental acclimatization
15. Bergmann's
16. Allen's
17. allometry
18. Sociobiology
19. altruism
20. inclusive fitness
21. kin selection
22. parental investment
23. Ethology
24. indirect bias
25. group selection
26. anagenesis
27. phyletic gradualism
28. cladogenesis
29. punctuated equilibrium
30. Species selection

Multiple Choice Questions

1. b
2. d
3. c
4. a
5. a
6. c
7. b
8. c
9. a
10. b

Chapter 4: The Primates

STUDY STRATEGY: HOW TO PREPARE FOR AN ESSAY EXAMINATION

Psyching Out The Professor: Or, What Is The Essay Really Supposed To Be About?

Questions for essay examinations tend to be very broad and general. This may cause inexperienced essay writers to panic. What can that professor possibly be thinking to ask a question like "Discuss the relationship between kinship and biology." A student may reason, "To answer this question correctly, I would need to write a whole book! But the professor knows I can only write a few paragraphs. So this must be a trick question. I've got to figure out what the professor is really after."

Some questions do require you to keep your wits about you. But in general the fear of broad essay questions, and the conviction that the professor must really be after something other than what the question asks for, is misplaced. Most essay questions are broad for a reason, but that reason is not "to trap students." A broad essay topic may make it easier for you to write a good essay. Asking you to "discuss" a broad topic is a graceful way of asking you to write down, in as full and orderly a way as possible, all you know about the topic in question. You have the freedom, under the umbrella of a broad essay topic, to decide on an approach to the topic, collect as much relevant information as you can, organize it to the best of your ability, and write about it as clearly and logically as you can. You have the freedom to show the instructor how much you know and how well you know it, in the best English you can muster

There is another area of freedom for students in an essay exam. Look again at the question mentioned above: Discuss the relationship between kinship and biology. To answer this question, one student may decide to write about the relationship between different marriage patterns and biology, saying little about descent. A second student, however, may choose to emphasize the relationship between different patterns of descent and biology, saying little about marriage. If both essays are well-written and full of relevant information, both would be "A" essays, even though they didn't answer the question in exactly the same way. This is what people mean when they sometimes say that there is "no single right answer" to an essay question. The broader the essay question, the more room there is for students to write essays that reflect what they know best.

Tips for Preparing for Essay Exams

1. *Do all the assigned readings, attend all classes, and take good notes.*
   This should go without saying.
2. *Review your notes often.*
   Writing an essay test requires you to recall information, and it can be difficult to recall information if you have not reviewed often.
3. *Attempt to predict test questions.*
   Some hints on ways to predict essay questions include the following:
   - Review the syllabus. Are there major concepts that stand out?
   - Review your notes. Are there major concepts or points that stand out?
   - Review the outline of the chapters in the table of contents and chapter summaries of your textbook. What major concepts or points would make good essay questions?
   - Talk with students who had the class before. What possible test questions would they suggest?

4. *Go through your notes and readings, looking for material relevant to the questions you predicted.*
   Write down information that should be part of your answer. Check for overlap between class notes and assigned readings. Write down definitions for all technical terms. Write down details concerning examples you wish to use to illustrate your answer, so that the examples will be complete and convincing.
5. *Think about the material you have gathered and its relation to the question.*
   What information is the most important? Least important? Which examples are strongest? Where would the examples best fit into your essay answer?
6. *Organize your answer.*
   Think of an essay as having three parts: introduction, body, and conclusion. The introduction may consist of only a few sentences in which you summarize the main points to be developed in the body of the essay. The body should be the logical presentation of information gathered from notes and readings that justifies your answer. The conclusion need be only one or two sentences that tie up loose ends and restate the major points of your essay.
7. *Practice writing your essays ahead of time.*
   Study after study has shown that the more you write, the better a writer you become. Practicing writing out your essays will also give you a chance to see just how sure you are of your arguments and where you need further work. Finally, writing things down is an excellent way to lodge them in your memory.
8. *Proofread your essays and evaluate your answers for content and structure.*
   Content: Did you include all the arguments, concepts, details, examples, and illustrations?
   Structure: Did you include an introduction? Are the main ideas, details, and examples in the body of the essay clearly delineated by paragraphs? Did the ideas flow from one idea to the next? If appropriate, did you use transitional words such as "first," "second," "third"? Did you include a brief summary?

If you have written and proofread practice essays in preparation for the exam, you will discover that test-taking anxiety virtually disappears the day of the test. All the hard work will have been completed before you even walk into the classroom

Tips for Writing Your Essay Answer in Class

1. *Read each question carefully.*
   Be sure you understand what is being asked of you. Some essay questions are short and broad in scope: "Discuss the relationship between kinship and biology." Other questions may have several parts to them: "The anthropological perspective is described in your text as holistic, comparative, and evolutionary. What does this mean? What are the subfields of anthropology? What is the role of each subfield in the integrated study of human beings that is anthropology?" Write down all the parts of the question that need to be answered, so that you do not overlook any of them. In this case, you might write a question-inspired outline as follows:
   A. Define holistic, comparative, evolutionary.
   B. List the subfields of anthropology.
   C. What is the role of each subfield in anthropology, as an integrated study?
   In all cases, write down terms that need to be defined, as well as possible examples that could illustrate your answer.
2. *Evaluate your answer. Assume you are the teacher grading this essay.*
   Did you write an introduction? Did the body of your essay include all the required points, details, and examples? Did you answer every part of the question? Do the ideas flow in a logical manner? Did you write a conclusion?
3. *Do not assume that the reader of your essay knows more than you do.*
   Students who forget to define their terms or illustrate with examples sometimes plead, "But I knew the instructor would know what I meant!" True enough— the instructor does know what technical terms

mean, and which examples are relevant. But the essay exam is supposed to show the instructor that you know what the terms and examples mean and that you can use them properly! As high school math teachers always say, "Show your work!"

4. *In conclusion, think of each essay question as a chance for you to tell your instructor everything you think is important about the topic.*

   This means giving evidence that you have done the assigned readings and attended the relevant lectures, by making clear reference to the material covered in them. Nothing is more disappointing than an essay that attempts to answer the question using "common sense"—that is, an essay that shows no evidence that its writer ever opened the textbook or attended a single day of class, even if she or he has done both. Include as much detail and as many appropriate concrete examples as you can cram into the four or five paragraphs you will write.

After the Test: What Do I Do now?

When you receive your test scores, you may be thrilled and delighted; you may, however, be disappointed with your score. Frustrated? Develop a plan.

1. *Analyze your answer.*
   If the instructor wrote comments on the paper, try to discern from the comments why you received that score. Think about the two areas: content and structure. Were you missing major ideas, details, illustrations, or examples? Did you answer every part of the question? Evaluate the structure of the answer. Did you have an introduction? Did the information in the body of your essay flow logically from one idea to the next? If applicable, did you use paragraphs and signal words ("first," "second," "third") to lead the reader from one point to the next? Did you include a summary?

2. *Discuss your test with your instructor.*
   Definitely see your instructor if he or she did not make comments on your paper. Some instructors just mark down a score, and you may not be able to determine why that particular score was given. Ask the instructor for suggestions so you can improve your score on the next test.

3. *Review how to prepare for and write essays.*
   Go back and reread this chapter's *Tips for Preparing for Essay Exams* and *Tips For Writing Your Essay Answer in Class*. In addition, consider seeing a tutor for help in predicting questions, writing essay answers, and evaluating the structure and content of your answers.

It is not easy to analyze your essay test when you receive a low score. However, knowing your strengths and weaknesses can help you do better in the future. Hang in there!

EXERCISES

Key Terms Review

Use the appropriate key term(s) in each sentence that follows.

affiliation
analogy
anthropoids
anthropomorphism
clade
cladistics
dentition
diurnal
dominance hierarchy
ecological niche

grade
grooming behavior
hominids
hominoids
homology
infanticide
morphology
mya
nocturnal
phenetics

prehensile
prosimians
sexual dimorphism
sexual selection
socioecology
stereoscopic vision
taxon
taxonomy
theory of optimal foraging

1. _____ is the physical shape and size of an organism or its body parts.

2. The attribution of human characteristics to animals is known as _____.

3. A form of vision in which the visual field of each eye of a two-eyed (binocular) animal overlaps, producing depth perception, is known as _____.

4. The ability to grasp makes an animal's fingers, toes, or tail _____.

5. _____ animals are active during the day, while those who are _____ are active during the night.

6. A biological classification of various kinds of organisms is called a _____, while each species or group of related species, at any level in the classification, is called a

   _____.

7. The comparison of physical (or phenotypic) similarities to create biological taxonomies is known as

   _____.

8. A _____ is a level of taxonomic classification that groups organisms that seem to have developed similar adaptations at a similar level of complexity in similar environments.

9. _____ are "pre-monkeys": the least complex grade of primates who resemble, more closely than any other living primates, the earliest primates to have evolved from mammalian ancestors.

10. The grade of primate evolution that includes monkeys, apes, and humans is the

    _____.

11. The more advanced grade of primate evolution that includes apes and humans is called

    _____.

12. The abbreviation for "million years ago" is _____.

13. The members of the most advanced grade of primate evolution that includes humans and near-humans such as the australopithecines are called _____.

14. A(n) _____ is a taxonomic term that describes physical similarity based on genetic inheritance due to common descent, while a(n) _____ is a taxonomic term that describes a physical similarity due to convergent or parallel evolution, as when two species with highly disparate evolutionary histories develop similar physical features as a result of having to adapt to a similar environment.

15. A method of classifying biological organisms based on evolutionary relatedness alone is called

    _____.

16. A _____ is a taxonomic classification of a group of organisms possessing a set of shared, derived features.

17. Any species' way of life—what it eats and how it finds mates, raises its young, relates to companions, and protects itself from predators—is its _____.

18. _____ refers to the size, shape, and number of teeth that characterize a particular species or organism.

19. The observable phenotypic differences between males and females of the same species are called

    _____.

20. _____ is the selective pressure acting on males who must compete with one another for access to females.

21. The deliberate killing of unweaned offspring is called _____.

22. _____ is an approach to primate studies that tries to explain different forms of primate society by relating them to the different environments in which each primate species typically lives, and to the food it typically eats.

23. The _____ is a theory predicting that a primate will maximize the amount and quality of food it eats, while minimizing the effort to find such food.

24. A _____ is the relative ranking of animals within a social group, based on the assumption that, especially among males, social organization is the outcome of struggles to dominate each other as well as females and younger animals.

25. Friendly interaction between animals, often measured by patterns of grooming, is called _____.

26. _____ consists of friendly interactions between primates, involving one primate parting the fur of another to remove parasites or bits of dead skin.

Multiple Choice Questions

1. Why is studying primates important to anthropologists?
   a. It is easier to study primates than people.
   b. Primates can offer insight into the evolutionary past of human beings.
   c. Primate behavior is fundamentally equivalent to human behavior.
   d. both b and c

2. Which of the following is NOT an ancestral characteristic of primates?
   a. presence of collar bone
   b. presence of five digits
   c. presence of vestigial tail
   d. plantigrade locomotion

3. Which of the following is NOT a primate grade?
   a. prosimians
   b. anthropoids
   c. hominoids
   d. humanoids

4. Where are most primates likely to be found?
   a. Australia
   b. coastal Africa
   c. temperate forests
   d. tropical rain forests

5. In which of the following prosimians are females individually dominant over males?
   a. lemurs
   b. lorises
   c. tarsiers
   d. bush babies

6. New World monkeys differ from Old World monkeys in which of the following ways?
   a. nose shape
   b. dentition
   c. prehensile tail
   d. all of the above

7. Sociobiological analyses of gray langur behavior claim that _____.
    a. infanticide makes sense as a reproductive strategy for males
    b. female "investment" in one's offspring is just as important as male "investment"
    c. not enough is known to draw meaningful conclusions about differential parental investment
    d. infanticide is maladaptive

8. The smallest of the apes is the _____.
    a. chimpanzee
    b. gibbon
    c. gorilla
    d. orangutan

9. Socioecological studies have directed researchers' attention to _____.
    a. the importance of the environment in primate behavior
    b. the size of primate teeth in relation to body weight
    c. less than optimal behavior
    d. all of the above

10. A male baboon has been observed defending its group, breaking up fights between other group members, and leading group movement. These characteristics might lead a primatologist to conclude that this baboon is _____.
    a. affiliated
    b. dominant
    c. monogamous
    d. submissive

11. Recent research on primates has emphasized _____.
    a. the flexibility of primate behavior
    b. the importance of primate social relationships
    c. the role of genetic inheritance in aggression
    d. both a and b

Arguing Anthropology

Questions for discussion and thought:

1. Chimpanzees are so similar to human beings that they have often been used as human stand-ins for experimentation or for testing medications. Is this ethical?

2. What (if anything) can the evidence for aggression and affiliation among nonhuman primates tell us about ourselves?

ANSWER KEY

Key Terms Review

1. Morphology
2. anthropomorphism
3. stereoscopic vision
4. prehensile
5. Diurnal; nocturnal
6. taxonomy; taxon
7. phenetics
8. grade
9. Prosimians
10. anthropoids
11. hominoids
12. mya
13. hominids
14. homology; analogy
15. cladistics
16. clade
17. ecological niche
18. Dentition
19. sexual dimorphism
20. sexual selection
21. infanticide
22. socioecology
23. theory of optimal foraging
24. dominance hierarchy
25. affiliation
26. Grooming behavior

Multiple Choice Questions

1. b
2. c
3. d
4. d
5. a
6. d
7. c
8. b
9. a
10. b
11. d

Chapter 5: Studying the Human Past

STUDY STRATEGY: ORGANIZING INFORMATION AND MAKING CONNECTIONS

One of my tutors was helping a student prepare for a lengthy, difficult test. She told the student she had taken the course during her first quarter and spent hours studying for the midquarter test. Unfortunately, when answering the test questions, she became confused regarding what information went with each historical time period, and she couldn't remember other information. She said her grade had been terrible and had certainly not reflected the amount of time she had studied. She explained that she had analyzed the way she studied and believed she had seen the information as separate pieces, instead of organizing the information so she could focus on the relationship between concepts. For example, she said she could have made a chart for each time period (e.g. Greek, Roman) and included information she needed to know (e.g. dates, writers, types of plays). For the final test she had changed her study strategy and made note cards and charts, thinking about the information and the relationship between ideas. Her final went well, so she passed the class with a good mark.

When preparing for tests, you obviously have to know all the ideas, facts and examples. Successful students go beyond this step; they organize the information and think about the connections between ideas. These students generally have a higher comfort level when taking their tests.

Making Connections by Using Charts

Organizing information into a chart can help you make connections. To see this, read the section on Dating Methods and complete the following charts.

1. Dating Methods				
Method	Page Number	Description	Advantages	Disadvantages
Relative Dates				
Chronometric Dates				

2. Relative Dating Methods					
Method	Page Number	Description	Examples	Advantages	Disadvantages
Stratigraphic Superposition					
Fluorine Method					
Biostrati-graphic Dating					

3. Radiometric Dating Methods of Chronometric Dating					
Method	Page Number	Description	Examples	Advantages	Disadvantages
Potassium Argon					
Fission-Track					
Uranium Series					
Radiocarbon Dating					
Thermo-luminescence					

4. Non-Radiometric Dating Methods of Chronometric Dating					
Method	Page Number	Description	Examples	Advantages	Disadvantages
Dendro-chronology					
Paleomag-netism					
Biomolecular Clock					

There are several advantages to charting. First, you have generated questions: What is the description of dendrochronology? What are the advantages and disadvantages of using the dendrochronology method of dating? Second, you can compare and contrast the concepts (in this case dating methods). This helps you to recognize the relationship between the methods. Organizing information into a chart is a form of active study. You must attend to and concentrate on the information, thus increasing the probability that you will recall the information. However, to ensure that you remember the dating methods for your test, review often. Quiz yourself by asking questions; look away and answer your questions.

Note: There is a hominid evolution chart that you may find useful on page 51 of this Study Guide.

EXERCISES

Key Terms Review

Use the appropriate key term(s) in each sentence that follows.

archaeological culture
archaeological record
artifacts
assemblage
biostratigraphic dating
chronometric
cross-cutting relationships
ethnoarchaeology
excavation

features
feminist archaeology
historical archaeology
nonradiometric
radiometric
region
relative
seriation

site
stratum
superposition
survey
taphonomy

1. Objects that have been deliberately and intelligently shaped by human or near-human activity are called _____.

2. The _____ consists of the assemblage of material objects constructed by humans or near-humans.

3. Dating methods that arrange material evidence in a linear sequence, with each object in the sequence being identified as older or younger in relation to another object are called _____.

4. Dating methods based on laboratory techniques that assign ages in years to material evidence are called _____.

5. A _____ is a layer; in geologic terms, it is a layer of rock and soil.

6. The law of _____ is a principle of geological interpretation stating that layers lower down in a sequence of strata must be older than the layers above them, and, therefore, that objects embedded in lower layers must be older than objects embedded in upper layers.

7. The law of _____ is a principle of geologic interpretation stating that in places where old rocks are crosscut by other geologic features, the intruding features must be younger than the layers of rock they cut across.

8. _____ is a relative dating method that relies on patterns of fossil distribution in different rock layers.

9. _____ is a relative dating method based on the assumption that artifacts that look alike must have been made at the same time.

10. Chronometric dating methods based on scientific knowledge about the rate at which various radioactive isotopes of naturally occurring elements transform themselves into other elements by losing subatomic particles are known as _____.

11. Chronometric dating methods that do not use rates of nuclear decay to assign ages in years to material evidence are known as _____.

12. A precise geographical location of the remains of past human activity is a _____.

13. The precise geographical locations of a series of sites are grouped together in a _____.

14. Nonportable remnants from the past, such as house walls or ditches, are called _____.

15. _____ is the study of the way present-day societies use artifacts and structures on the sites where they live and the way these objects become part of the archaeological record.

16. The study of the various processes that bones and stones undergo in the course of becoming part of the fossil and archaeological records is known as _____.

17. In archaeology, a(n) _____ is the physical examination of a geographical region in which promising sites are most likely to be found.

18. The systematic uncovering of archaeological remains through the removal of the deposits of soil and other material covering them and accompanying them is called a(n) _____.

19. The grouping together of artifacts and structures from a particular time and place in a site is a(n)

_____.

20. _____ is the term used to describe the grouping together of similar assemblages found at several sites.

21. The research approach known as _____ actively explores the reason that why women's contributions have been systematically written out of the archaeological record and suggests new approaches to the human past that will allow such contributions to be written back in.

22. The study of archaeological sites associated with written records, frequently the study of post-European contact sites in the world is known as _____.

Multiple Choice Questions

1. The archaeological record consists of _____.
   a. stone tools
   b. ideas and interpretations of the way people lived in ancient civilizations
   c. material evidence of human modifiation of the material environment over time
   d. the study of the human past in all its forms

2. The dating method that identifies a particular object as older or younger in relation to some other object is called _____.
   a. absolute dating
   b. biostratigraphic dating
   c. chronometric dating
   d. relative dating

3. Which of the following dating methods would be best for dating material that is between 150,000 and 300,000 years old?
   a. Dendrochronology
   b. Potassium-Argon
   c. Radiocarbon
   d. Uranium-Series

4. A major difference between archaeology and treasure-hunting is that archaeologists _____.
   a. are interested in the context in which artifacts are found
   b. are only interested in recovering objects that show high levels of technical skill and aesthetic achievement
   c. try to discover ancient civilizations
   d. work during the day in well-defined, protected areas

5. You have been studying an archaeological site in which a variety of stone tools has been found. Can you conclude that the people who inhabited the site did not use bone tools or wooden tools?
   a. Yes; there are none at the site.
   b. Yes; bone and wooden tools leave some indication behind.
   c. No; people who used stone tools always used bone and wood.
   d. No; bone and wooden tools used at the site may have decayed.

6. The most common archaeological survey technique is _____.
   a. using a surveyor's transit and a view camera
   b. walking over a field and looking at the ground
   c. using satellite-generated survey maps to identify likely sites
   d. Using a hand-held video camera from a reasonable height

7. The systematic uncovering of archaeological remains through the removal of covering material is called _____.
   a. archaeological culture
   b. excavation
   c. revelation
   d. surveying

8. Artifacts from a particular time and place in a site, grouped together, form a(n) _____.
   a. archaeological culture
   b. assemblage
   c. excavation
   d. record

9. A feminist archaeological approach to the analysis of a site would most likely involve consideration of _____.
   a. possible social relations at the site
   b. the possible activities of the women living at the site
   c. ethnoarchaeological evidence concerning gender and tool use
   d. all of the above

   In Chapter 3, Microevolution and Macroevolution: Human Evolution in the Short and Long Term, we discussed analogy questions. Remember, to solve an analogy question, you have to recognize the relationship between the ideas, people, events, or things. Here is another analogy question:

10. With regard to dating, Absolute:Relative::
    a. Chronometric:Seriation
    b. Superposition:Crosscutting Relationships
    c. Radiocarbon:Potassium-Argon
    d. Fluorine Method:Thermoluminescence
In this question, you need to remember which dating methods are absolute and which are relative. Each answer has two different forms of dating methods but only one answer has one absolute and one relative method.

Arguing Anthropology

Questions for discussion and thought:

1. In recent years, state and federal laws have mandated that the remains of indigenous people of North America found in archaeological or scientific collections be returned to contemporary indigenous peoples or appropriate agencies so that those remains can be reburied. Are there any circumstances in which archaeological excavations of human burials is justifiable?

2. Since archaeological excavation destroys the past as it reveals it, should archaeologists stop excavating until better nondestructive technologies are developed?

ANSWER KEYS

Key Terms Review	Multiple Choice Questions
1. artifacts	1. c
2. archaeological record	2. c
3. relative	3. d
4. chronometric	4. a
5. stratum	5. d
6. superposition	6. b
7. crosscutting relationships	7. b
8. Biostratigraphic dating	8. b
9. Seriation	9. d
10. radiometric	10. a
11. nonradiometric	
12. site	
13. region	
14. features	
15. Ethnoarchaeology	
16. taphonomy	
17. survey	
18. excavation	
19. assemblage	
20. Archaeological culture	
21. feminist archaeology	
22. historical archaeology	

Chapter 6: Primate Evolution

STUDY STRATEGY: ORGANIZING INFORMATION AND MAKING CONNECTIONS II

Authors: Organizing Information to Help Students Make Connections

The authors of this textbook help you to make connections. For example, the introduction to this chapter on primate evolution, Approaching the Fossil Record, makes a connection with the previous chapter. The authors tell you what was discussed in the last chapter and what will be the new and more complicated material concerning the classification of primate fossils in this chapter.

> Chapter 5 reviewed a variety of impressive, systematic techniques of survey and excavation that professional paleoanthropologists rely on to reconstruct human origins. The meaningful interpretations they wrest from the fragmentary evidence they recover is truly impressive. At first glance, it would appear that classifying fossils is a relatively straightforward activity: simply grouping together the bones and teeth that resemble one another and applying a species label. However, the classification is more problematic than this for at least two reasons.

Another way the authors help you to make connections is by using signal words ("first," "second," "because," "in addition," "another," "for example"). In the introduction the authors discuss the problems of classifying fossils, and they use signal words to help you follow their flow of thought. Note the bold print emphasizing the signal words in the paragraph you've just looked at and in the following examples.

Second Paragraph: "First, it is not always clear what the similarities and the differences between fossils indicate. . . ."

Third Paragraph: "Second, it is not always clear that fossil species boundaries coincide with major morphological differences. Eldredge and Tattersall. . . ."

Because of the signal words, you can connect the first reason in the second paragraph with the second reason from the third paragraph. You can generate your own question: What are the two reasons for problems in classifying fossils? If the following question appeared on your test, you would know the answer is "D".

Classifying species can be a problem because _____.
a. there may be different interpretations of fossil remains
b. because of dating techniques, there are very limited problems in classifying fossil remains
c. fossil remains (e.g., bones) of different species may look similar to each other.
d. both a and b

To summarize, both the student-generated method of organizing information discussed in the previous chapter and the author-generated method can help you make connections so you can recognize the relationships between concepts.

EXERCISES

Key Terms Review

Use the appropriate key term(s) in each sentence that follows.

Aegyptopithecus　　　　　　　　　hominoids
bilophodont molars　　　　　　　　platyrrhines
catarrhines　　　　　　　　　　　　postcranial skeleton
cranium　　　　　　　　　　　　　primates of modern aspect
evolutionary mosaic　　　　　　　　*Proconsul*
holotype　　　　　　　　　　　　　Y-5 molar

1. The earliest fossil primates to resemble living, modern prosimians are called _____.

2. The _____ is composed of the bones of the head, excluding the jaw

3. The _____ is made up of the bones of the body, excluding those of the head.

4. The best or most complete examples of a particular fossil that are used as a standard against which future similar finds will be compared is called the _____.

5. _____ are Old World anthropoids, including Old World monkeys, apes, and humans.

6. _____ are New World anthropoids: all species of New World monkeys.

7. The largest of the Oligocene fossil anthropoids is known as _____.

8. The _____ is an Old World anthropoid cheek tooth with a distinctive surface pattern of five cusps that are separated by a distinctly shaped furrow.

9. Old World cercopithecoid molars with four cusps arranged in pairs, with each pair of cusps joined by a ridge of enamel called a *loph*, are called _____.

10. _____ form the grade of primate evolution that includes apes and humans.

11. A genus of early African hominoid fossils is the _____.

12. A(n) _____ is a phenotypic pattern that shows how different traits of an organism, responding to different selections pressures, may evolve at different rates.

Multiple Choice Questions

1. Classification of fossils is problematic because it is not always clear _____.
    a. what the similarities and differences between fossils indicate
    b. where the fossils came from
    c. where the classification comes from
    d. who is doing the classifying

2. The primate order is thought to have appeared about _____.
    a. 80 million years ago
    b. 65 million years ago
    c. 40 million years ago
    d. 27 million years ago

3. Primates have retained many specific body parts that other mammals have lost during their evolution. This makes primates _____ organisms.
    a. adapted
    b. generalized
    c. holotypic
    d. specialized

4. The first primates of modern aspect LEAST resembled which of the following modern primates?
    a. baboons
    b. lemurs
    c. lorises
    d. tarsiers

5. *Aegyptopithecus* is an important fossil to physical anthropologists because _____.
    a. it is the likely ancestor of the primates
    b. it is better known than any other Eocene fossil
    c. it is the likely ancestor of Old World anthropoids
    d. it has bilophodont molars, which indicate that it is very old

6. In the past, many experts believed that Old World and New World monkeys had evolved separately. Which of the following is NOT one of their reasons?
    a. Old World and New World monkeys are quite distinct morphologically.
    b. Speciation was understood in terms of phyletic gradualism.
    c. Biochemical studies show that New World anthropoids are closer to prosimians than to Old World anthropoids.
    d. There were other groups of animals that were believed to have evolved similarly.

7. The first hominoid fossils date to the _____ period.
    a. Paleocene
    b. Eocene
    c. Oligocene
    d. Miocene

8. The present understanding of the status of *Sivapithecus* holds that it was _____.
   a. an early ancestor of the modern orangutan
   b. ancestral to the hominid line
   c. an evolutionary dead end
   d. an example of the Asian, rather than the African, origins of hominoids

9. Some argue that the common ancestor of chimpanzees, gorillas, and human beings would have resembled hominids more closely than modern apes. This implies that _____.
   a. modern apes are more advanced than modern human beings
   b. hominids are more generalized than apes
   c. apes are descended from hominids
   d. all of the above

10. The earliest prehominids looked like _____.
   a. gorillas
   b. Miocene apes
   c. Miocene cercopithecoids
   d. Lemurs

Arguing Anthropology

Questions for discussion and thought:

1. What good is fossil evidence?

2. The concept of an "evolutionary mosaic" is a provocative and powerful one. Why?

ANSWER KEY

Key Terms Review

1. primates of modern aspect
2. cranium
3. postcranial skeleton
4. holotype
5. Catarrhines
6. Platyrrhines
7. *Aegyptopithecus*
8. Y-5 molar
9. bilophodont molars
10. Hominoids
11. *Proconsul*
12. evolutionary mosaic

Multiple Choice Questions

1. a
2. b
3. b
4. a
5. c
6. c
7. d
8. a
9. b
10. b

Chapter 7: Hominid Evolution

STUDY STRATEGY: NOTE-TAKING

Completing the questions in this Study Guide is an excellent way to prepare for your examinations. The majority of your test questions may come from the textbook; however, other questions will come from your notes. In addition, your instructor may expect you to include information from your notes when writing your essay answers. Therefore, let's discuss note-taking from classroom lectures and discussions.

Questions, Problems, Solutions

Following are some student analyses of note-taking and related problems and solutions. As you read this section, see if any of the students' comments also pertain to you.

Problem with Instructor's Lecture Speed:
"My instructor talks too fast. I have a horrible time writing all the information in my notes."

Possible Solutions:
1. Read the assignments before class, so you will be familiar with the information. This mental preparation will make note-taking easier. When the majority of the information flying rapidly past your ear is new, it is difficult to take notes fast enough. However, when you know some of the information, it is easier to take notes selectively, on the information you do not know. In some situations you may even revise your opinion and think the instructor is not such a "motor mouth."
2. Abbreviate information; for example,
   - anth = anthropology
   - gen = generally
   - Eng = England
   When reviewing your notes after class, think about words which can be abbreviated.
3. Do the best you can with taking notes in class. After class, cross-check your notes with class-mates. Two or more sets of notes are better than one set.
4. Make an appointment to talk with your instructor personally. Sometimes people do not realize how fast they are talking. Consider whether it would help to say something like, "Although I study the chapters before coming to class, I have a difficult time taking notes because you often speak rather rapidly." If at all possible, tell the instructor instances where note-taking was more comfortable for you. For example, "At times you pause, and that makes it easier to take notes. It also helps when you write on the board or use transparencies." Instructors are usually sensitive to students' comfort levels and will try to make the learning environment as positive as possible.

Problem with Attention in Class
"I daydream or fall asleep because I have a hard time paying attention. What can I do to improve my concentration in class?"

Possible Solutions
1. Often boredom leads to daydreaming and falling asleep. So how can you create an interest in the course? One way is to make the class relevant to your life now or to your life in the future. How can an anthropological perspective help you if you're going into personnel management? Eco-

nomics? Accounting? How can the material you are learning in class apply to current international crises or national controversies?
2. Ask questions and participate in the class discussions.
3. Plan to take lots of notes even if you do not need to take notes. It is difficult to write and sleep at the same time. So write!
4. Every time you catch yourself drifting off, put a check mark on the top of your notes. Make a commitment to decrease the number of check marks you make during succeeding class hours.

Problem with Note-Taking
"I don't know what to write in my notes because I can't tell the important information."

Possible Solutions
1. Reading the assigned information before class may help you recognize the main concepts and relevant details.
2. After class, cross check your notes with other students so you can get an idea of what others think is important.
3. Make an appointment to talk with your instructor and discuss your notes. Ask the instructor to go over your notes with you to determine whether you are capturing the appropriate information.

Problem with Discussion
"Our class is mostly discussion. It's lots of fun, but I don't have many notes, and now the instructor said the test was over the book and our notes."

Possible Solutions
1. Try the best you can during class to take notes. After class, think about the discussion and write a summary.
   * What was the topic we discussed today?
   * What were the major points we discussed about this topic?
   * What were the relevant details and examples?

   Such a "journal" of information you discuss each day can be an effective supplement to your notes.
2. Form a study group and make a list of the important topics, main ideas, details and examples covered in class. Try to predict test questions from this information. The study group is also an excellent place to discuss the Arguing Anthropology questions from this Study Guide.

Note: A table for reviewing the hominids is on page 51.

EXERCISES

Key Term Review

Use the appropriate key term(s) in each sentence that follows.

Acheulean tradition
Asian chopper/chopping tool
  assemblages
basicranial flexion
bipedalism
breccia
cores
cranial capacity
diastema

Early Stone Age
flakes
foraging societies
gracile australopithecines
hominids
Homo erectus
Homo habilis
Lower Paleolithic
masseter

morphological space
Oldowan tradition
postorbital constriction
robust australopithecines
sagittal crest
taphonomy
temporal muscle
valgus angle
zygomatic arch

1. Habitual upright locomotion on two feet is called _____.

2. _____ are bipedal hominoids: the most advanced grade of primate evolution, which includes humans and near-humans, such as the australopithecines.

3. The angle of the femur pointing inward toward the knee joint is the _____.

4. The space in the tooth row of the opposite jaw for each canine to fit into when the jaws are closed is the

    _____.

5. Members of the species *Australopithecus africanus* that had small and lightly built faces are called

    _____.

6. Members of the species *Australopithecus robustus* (or *Australopithecus boisei*) dating from about 2.5 to 1

    mya, that had rugged jaws, flat faces, and enormous molars are known as

    _____.

7. _____ measures the size of the braincase.

8. The _____ muscle is responsible for moving the jaw that attaches to the

    cheekbone.

9. The _____ is the cheekbone.

10. The _____ muscle, responsible for moving the jaw, passes under the

    cheekbone, and attaches at the top of the skull.

11. The bony ridge along the midline of the skull to which jaw muscles are attached is the

    _____.

12. _____ is a mixture of hardened sediments and fossils that do not show

    stratigraphy, making it difficult for scientists to date the fossils it contains.

13. _____ is a measurement of the degree of morphological difference between two fossil organisms.

14. The species of large-brained gracile hominids 2 million years old and younger is called

_____.

15. The narrowing of the skull behind the ridges of bone that form the eye orbits is called

_____.

16. _____ are rocks or pebbles from which _____ are removed during stone-tool manufacture and that may or may not have been used as tools.

17. A stone-tool tradition named after the Olduvai Gorge (Tanzania) where the first specimens of the oldest human artifacts (2.5 to 2 mya) were found has been named _____.

18. _____ is the study of the various processes that bones and stones undergo in the course of becoming part of the fossil and archaeological records.

19. Human groups who neither farm nor herd but make a living by relying on a variety of foods that can be collected or caught in the environments they inhabit are known as _____.

20. The species of large-brained, robust hominids that lived between 0.8 mya and 0.4 mya is called

_____.

21. _____ refers to the sharpness of the angle with which the rear surface of the palate reaches upward from the front edge of the foramen magnum.

22. A Lower Paleolithic stone-tool tradition associated with *Homo erectus* and characterized by stone bifaces, or hand axes is called _____.

23. The name given to the period of Oldowan and Acheulean stone-tool traditions in Europe is the

_____.

24. The name given to the period of Oldowan and Acheulean stone-tool traditions in Africa is the

_____.

25. A stone-tool tradition in Asia, associated with the same time period as the Lower Paleolithic in Europe and the early Stone Age in Africa is known as the _____.

Multiple Choice Questions

1. What form of locomotion sets hominids apart from other hominoids?
   a. bipedalism
   b. knuckle walking
   c. plantigrade locomotion
   d. quadrupedalism

2. Which of the following is NOT a significant evolutionary change in hominids?
   a. brain expansion
   b. reliance on culture
   c. dentition
   d. prehensile hand

3. It has been suggested that early bipedal hominids might have been _____.
   a. endurance hunters and gatherers
   b. local area foragers
   c. large mammal hunters
   d. skilled high-speed scavengers

4. The hominid bipedal adaptation seems to illustrate the importance of _____.
   a. environmental changes
   b. diet
   c. variation
   d. all of the above

5. Which is the correct chronological order of Australopithecine species?
   a. *A. africanus*; *A. robustus*; *A. afarensis*
   b. *A. robustus*; *A. afarensis*; *A. africanus*
   c. *A. afarensis*; *A. aethiopicus*; *A. robustus*
   d. *A. africanus*; *A. afarensis*; *A. robustus*

6. What is the most striking difference between *Homo habilis* and *Australopithecus africanus*?
   a. body size
   b. the structure of the knee
   c. the size of the brain relative to body size
   d. the fully upright bipedalism, allowing for hunting and scavenging on the savannah

7. The oldest stone tools are at least how old?
   a. 6.5 million years old
   b. 2.5 million years old
   c. 1.4 million years old
   d. 675,000 years old

8. Models from primatology suggest that the social life of early human ancestors _____.
   a. was aggressive and male-dominant
   b. was peaceful and egalitarian
   c. was more like that of chimpanzees than of baboons
   d. was not identical to that of any modern primate species

9. Basicranial flexion in *Homo erectus* is _____ than that in *Homo habilis* and _____ than that in *Homo sapiens*, meaning that *H. erectus* could, at least to some extent, _____.
   a. greater; less; speak
   b. less; greater; hunt
   c. less; greater; speak
   d. greater; less; hunt

10. Evidence for *Homo erectus* hunting _____.
    a. tends to indicate that they relied on bows and arrows
    b. tends to indicate regular big-game hunting
    c. tends to indicate dependence on small-animal hunting
    d. has been questioned by taphonomists

Arguing Anthropology

Questions for discussion and thought:

1. Why should anyone care whether our ancestors hunted or scavenged?

2. Given the evidence in the text, which scenarios of early hominid life seem most reasonable to you? Why?

ANSWER KEY

Key Terms Review

1. bipedalism
2. Hominids
3. valgus angle
4. diastema
5. gracile australopithecines
6. robust australopithecines
7. Cranial capacity
8. masseter
9. zygomatic arch
10. temporal muscle
11. sagittal crest
12. Breccia
13. Morphological space
14. *Homo habilis*
15. postorbital constriction
16. Cores, flakes
17. Oldowan tradition
18. Taphonomy
19. foraging societies
20. *Homo erectus*
21. Basicranial flexion
22. Acheulean tradition
23. Lower Paleolithic
24. Early Stone Age
25. Asian chopper/chopping tool assemblages

Multiple Choice Questions

1. a
2. d
3. a
4. d
5. c
6. b
7. c
8. b
9. a
10. d

Hominid Worksheet

Hominid	Dates	Cranial Capacity	Dentition	Cranial and Post-Cranial Skeleton	Culture
Australopithecus					
A. afarensis					
A. aethiopicus					
A. robustus					
A. boisei					
Homo					
H. habilis					
H. erectus					
H. sapiens (archaic)					
H. sapiens (Neandertal)					
H. sapiens (modern)					

Chapter 8: The Evolution of *Homo Sapiens*

STUDY STRATEGY: ASKING QUESTIONS

Let's talk some more about the way questions help us concentrate on information as we read and study, and how asking and answering questions helps us understand and recall information.

Asking Questions to Improve Concentration and Comprehension

Textbook chapters can be so densely packed with information that it may be difficult to concentrate and to follow the flow of ideas. Asking your own questions as you read helps to keep you focused on the information and helps comprehension. You can also use the author's questions. The authors of this textbook are "reader friendly" because they often ask questions and then proceed to answer them. For example, in the section Archaic Homo Sapiens, the authors ask the following questions: "Do the fossils of archaic *H. sapiens* from Africa belong to a population directly ancestral to ourselves? And if they do, what is the status of the fossils from Europe and Asia that are also assigned to archaic *H. sapiens*?"

Next, the authors answer their questions. Keeping these questions in mind as you read can help you focus on the information, thus promoting active reading.

You could also rephrase the questions and ask other questions:

1. What are the fossils from Africa? What evidence do they provide that *Homo sapiens* from Africa are our ancestors?
2. What are the fossils from Europe and Asia? What do they tell us?
3. How do the fossils from Africa compare and contrast with the fossils from Europe and Asia?

Continue to develop other questions. For example, this section includes several names. As you read, you could write down the names and think about what each person believes about the above questions:

1. Günter Bräuer
2. Brian Fagan
3. G. Philip Rightmire
4. Richard Klein
5. Robert Foley
6. Milford Wolpoff

Answering Questions to Improve Comprehension and Recall

After you have finished reading, the next essential step is to stop and answer your questions and the authors' questions. Let's say you've finished reading the section, Archaic *Homo Sapiens*. Stop and answer the authors' questions and your questions to ensure that you understand and recall the information.

Students who do not stop to answer their questions often complain that they don't remember the information. Often these students did not focus their attention on what they were reading. We have all experienced situations in which we read five pages, but in actuality we only concentrated on three pages. We just pronounced the words for pages four and five; our minds were focusing on other things, such as a test we have to take, or the paper we have to write.

Students who complain that they can't remember what they are reading should change to the study strategy of asking questions, reading, and stopping to answer their questions. Some students may feel that this study strategy will take too much time. Any new behavior takes time—like fitting a new exercise program into a daily routine. However, once we are accustomed to doing something and the behavior becomes automatic, "time" does not seem to be such an issue. The behavior is just a natural part of our life.

Asking Questions to Prepare for Tests

Although asking any type of question as you read is helpful, some questions may be especially helpful for certain types of tests. Consider the following questions on the information in the Archaic *Homo Sapiens* section, which discusses the Out-of-Africa model and the regional continuity model.

1. What is the Out-of-Africa model?
2. What is the regional continuity model?
3. Compare and contrast the Out-of-Africa model with the regional continuity model.

Questions 1 and 2 are good because they require you to describe the main idea and details of each model. These questions would certainly prepare you for a multiple choice test. Question 3 requires you to know each model and, in addition, to think about the relationship between the two models. This sounds like an essay question.

Essay questions often require you to know the relationship (connection) between events, people, ideas, or things. Recognizing relationships (connections) is a higher-order thinking skill and can be a difficult task. However, when preparing for essay tests, an effective strategy is to ask questions which require you not only to recite the main ideas and facts, but to think and talk about the relationship between the ideas.

EXERCISES

Key Terms Review

Use the appropriate key term(s) in each sentence that follows.

anatomically modern *Homo sapiens*	Middle Stone Age
archaic *Homo sapiens*	Mousterian tradition
Aurignacian assemblages	Neandertals
blades	Out-of-Africa model
Broca's area	Paleoindians
Châtelperronian assemblages	pharynx
Clovis points	regional continuity model
Howieson's Poort Industry	Upper Paleolithic
intrusions	Wernicke's area
Late Stone Age	
Middle Paleolithic	

1. Hominids dating from 500,000 to 200,000 years ago that display both morphological features found in

    Homo erectus and morphological features common to *Homo sapiens* are known as _____.

2. The _____ is the hypothesis that only one subpopulation of *Homo erectus*, probably located in Africa, underwent a rapid spurt of evolution to produce *Homo sapiens* 200,000-100,000 years ago. After that time, *Homo sapiens* would itself have multiplied and moved out of Africa, gradually populating the globe and eventually replacing any remaining populations of *Homo erectus* or their descendants.

3. The _____ is the hypothesis that evolution from *Homo erectus* to *Homo sapiens* occurred gradually throughout the entire traditional range that *Homo erectus* occupied.

4. Hominid fossils assigned to the species *Homo sapiens*, with anatomical features similar to those of living human populations (short round skulls, small browridges and faces, prominent chins, and light skeletal build) are called _____.

5. _____ were a subspecies of *Homo sapiens* that lived in Europe and western Asia from 130,000 to 35,000 years ago.

6. The _____ is the muscle-walled space between the larynx and the soft palate.

7. _____ is the portion of the modern human brain that controls speech production.

8. _____ is the portion of the modern human brain that controls speech interpretation.

9. A Middle Paleolithic stone-tool tradition associated with Neandertals in Europe and Southwestern Asia and with anatomically modern human beings in Africa is the _____.

10. The name given to the period of Mousterian stone-tool tradition in Europe and southwestern Asia, 100,000 to 40,000 years ago, is _____.

11. The name given to the period of Mousterian stone-tool tradition in Africa, 100,000 to 40,000 years ago, is _____.

12. _____ are artifacts made by more recent populations that find their way into more ancient strata as the result of natural forces.

13. An artifact tradition dating from the Middle Stone Age in Africa that includes a number of backed tools that look like Late Stone Age blades is known as _____.

14. The name given to the period of highly elaborate stone-tool traditions in Europe in which blades were important, 40,000 to 10,300 years ago, is _____.

15. The period of highly elaborate stone tool traditions in Africa in which blades were important, 40,000 to 10,300 years ago, is known as _____.

16. _____ are stone tools that are at least twice as long as they are wide.

17. European Upper Paleolithic stone-tool assemblages dating 35,000 to 30,000 years ago that contain a mixture of typical Middle Paleolithic Mousterian backed knives and advanced pointed cutting tools called *burins* more typical of Upper Paleolithic assemblages are called _____.

18. Upper Paleolithic blade assemblages from Europe dating 34,000 to 30,000 years ago are called _____.

19. Anatomically modern human beings with Upper Paleolithic cultures, who were the first to move from Siberia into the Americas, are called _____.

20. _____ are the oldest stone tools in the New World, between 11,500 - 11,000 years old; they were finely made and probably hafted to shafts to make spears.

Multiple Choice Questions

1. Which of the following was the first hominid species to leave Africa?
   a. *Australopithecus africanus*
   b. *Homo habilis*
   c. *Homo erectus*
   d. *Homo sapiens*

2. Those who favor a punctuationist interpretation of the fossil record find that *Homo erectus* features were _____.
   a. stable for a long time and over a wide area
   b. gradually transformed into *Homo sapiens* features over an extended period of time
   c. quite close to *Homo sapiens* features
   d. stable for a long time only in Africa

3. The "Out-of-Africa" hypothesis holds that *Homo sapiens* originated _____.
   a. gradually throughout the *Homo erectus* range in Africa and Asia
   b. once, in Africa
   c. once, in Asia
   d. gradually throughout the *Homo erectus* range in Africa only

4. Which of the following is NOT a place where there were differences between Neandertals and anatomically modern human beings?
   a. chin
   b. brain size and shape
   c. bipedalism
   d. molars

5. At the present time, the best evidence for the "humanity" of the Neandertal is _____.
   a. burials
   b. care of injured, sick, and elderly
   c. cave bear cult
   d. ritual coloring of the body

6. The earliest anatomically modern fossils are about _____ years old.
   a. 15,000
   b. 55,000
   c. 105,000
   d. 170,000

7. What happened to the Neandertals?
   a. They were exterminated by more modern human beings.
   b. They interbred with modern human beings.
   c. They died out.
   d. No one is certain, although answers b and c seem more likely than a.

8. The earliest flowering of art in many forms is characteristic of which cultural tradition?
   a. Lower Paleolithic
   b. Mousterian
   c. Upper Paleolithic
   d. Neolithic

9. What kind of evidence is available for the transition from the Mousterian to the Upper Paleolithic?
   a. predominance of blade tools
   b. complex tools kits
   c. art
   d. all of the above

10. The best evidence for the earliest date of human settlement in the Americas is that for _____.
    a. 42,000 years ago
    b. 27,000 years ago
    c. 12,000 years ago
    d. 7,800 years ago

Arguing Anthropology

Questions for discussion and thought:

1. What's all the fuss about the area where the first *Homo sapiens* evolved? Why is it an issue?

2. At the end of this chapter, the authors write, "But one of the knottiest problems that remains concerns how we interpret mounting evidence that human biology and human culture evolved at different rates." Why is this problematic?

ANSWER KEY

Key Terms Review

1. archaic *Homo sapiens*
2. Out-of-Africa model
3. regional continuity model
4. anatomically modern *Homo sapiens*
5. Neandertals
6. pharynx
7. Broca's area
8. Wernicke's area
9. Mousterian tradition
10. Middle Paleolithic
11. Middle Stone Age
12. Intrusions
13. Howieson's Poort Industry
14. Upper Paleolithic
15. Late Stone Age
16. Blades
17. Châtelperronian assemblages
18. Aurignacian assemblages
19. Paleoindians
20. Clovis points

Multiple Choice Questions

1. c
2. a
3. b
4. c
5. b
6. c
7. d
8. c
9. d
10. c

Chapter 9: After the Ice Age: Sedentism, Domestication, and Agriculture

STUDY STRATEGY: MEMORY: VISUALIZING INFORMATION

Visualizing information may enhance your ability to understand and recall new material. The textbook includes numerous pictures, illustrations, and maps to help you visualize what you are reading. For example, in a previous chapter on hominid evolution and in this chapter, After the Ice Age: Sedentism, Domestication, and Agriculture, the pictures, illustrations, and maps vividly depict the information presented.

Strategies to Help Comprehension and Recall

1. Drawing pictures.
   If you are having a difficult time understanding what the authors are presenting and if they did not include a picture or illustration, try to draw a picture of what is happening.
2. Making visual images.
   While she was studying for her history test, one student pictured herself on a horse riding from town to town. She visualized what happened and who she talked to. Another student said that when he read biology, he would create a mental picture; for example, he mentally visualized how blood flows through the heart and lungs. This "active participation" helped both students understand and remember what was happening.
   Let's discuss an example from this chapter. In the second paragraph of the introduction, the authors discuss sedentism:

   > Sedentism (the process of increasingly permanent human habitation in one place) is "staying put," or settling down, and contrasts with the nomadic way of life of all human beings up until that point. As we shall see, sedentism is linked to the effects of the changing climate and to the domestication of plants.

   To make the definition more memorable, mentally visualize people settling down in one place, with plants growing around their village. The weather changes, but they adapt the way they live to the changes. This is an easy example; as you become proficient at visualizing, practice with more difficult examples.
3. Using descriptive writing to clarify difficult concepts.
   In the third paragraph in the section on animal domestication, the authors discuss types of changes:

   > Second, morphological changes occur in most animal populations as domestication progresses. There are changes in bone structure, as well. Wenke points out that the shape and size of sheep horns, for example, reflect the process of domestication (1990, 240). Wild sheep have larger, stronger horns than do domesticated sheep. . .

   If you did not know the meaning of morphological changes, the descriptive examples the authors present help you understand what the term means ("morph" means form). The descriptions also help you visualize the changes which occur, thus increasing your ability to recall the changes.

4. Using charts to visualize information.

In Chapter 5, the study strategy of organizing information into charts was discussed. Under the section on animal domestication, this chapter includes a chart summarizing the stages of animal-human relationships. Even though the text discussed the stages, it is helpful to see (visualize) the information summarized into a chart. This particular chart is also helpful because there is a lot of information in the paragraph on this subject.

Readers always notice the signal words of "first," "second," and "third." Sometimes, however, authors use other signal words, like "next" and "recent" to announce other stages. Readers need to translate these mentally into numbers. Also, if authors do not use numbers exclusively as signal words, some readers may miss points if they (or the authors) don't use a chart.

To summarize, memory is strengthened when more than one sense is involved in coding information for recall. Therefore, in addition to reciting and writing information, consider using visualizing techniques when you read and study.

EXERCISES

Key Terms Review

Use the appropriate key term(s) in each sentence that follows.

agriculture
broad spectrum foraging
chiefdom
domestication
monocropping

Natufian tradition
neolithic
sedentism
social stratification

1. The process of increasingly permanent human habitation in one place is known as _____.

2. _____ is human interference with the reproduction of another species, with the result that specific plants and animals become more useful to people and also dependent on them.

3. The systematic modification of the environments of plants and animals to increase their productivity and usefulness is known as _____.

4. An identifiable cultural tradition that developed in southwestern Asia about 12,500 years ago was the

_____.

5. A subsistence strategy based on collecting a wide range of plants and animals by hunting, fishing, and gathering is called _____.

6. _____ is a form of social organization in which people have unequal access to wealth, power, and prestige.

7. A _____ is a form of social organization in which a leader (the "chief") and his close relatives are set apart from the rest of the society and allowed privileged access to wealth, power, and prestige.

8. The _____ is the "New Stone Age," which began with the domestication of plants 10,300 years ago.

9. The practice of growing only one kind of plant in a field is known as _____.

Multiple Choice Questions

1. The process of increasingly permanent human habitation in one place is called _____.
   a. agriculture
   b. domestication
   c. sedentism
   d. transhumance

2. To be dispersed successfully by human beings, wild wheat requires _____.
   a. a brittle rachis
   b. a harder glume
   c. a small seed head
   d. seeds that mature at the same time

3. Which of the following is NOT evidence for animal domestication?
   a. presence of an animal species outside its natural range
   b. remains of animals of different ages and sexes at a site
   c. abrupt population increase of some species relative to others
   d. morphological changes in animal populations

4. Neighboring groups begin to compete with each other for prestige and fame. First, the members of one group invite the other group for a feast and give them valuables. Then, the members of the other group have to invite the first group for a feast and exchange. As this continues, more and more food is consumed and given away. To meet the needs for food, food production begins. Which of the following theories of agricultural development would best fit this scenario?
   a. the broad spectrum foraging argument
   b. the conflict argument
   c. the marginal zone argument
   d. the population argument

5. Which of the following is evidence that the Natufians lived in relatively permanent settlements?
   a. There are no young gazelle bones at the sites.
   b. There are permanent paths leading to and from settlement sites.
   c. There are cemeteries.
   d. all of the above

6. The appearance of domesticated plants is taken to be the end of one great cultural period and the beginning of another. The period that begins with domestication is called the _____.
   a. Neolithic
   b. Natufian
   c. Paleolithic
   d. Premodern

7. What is the relationship between sedentism and childbirth? With sedentism, _____.
   a. the birth rate increases
   b. the spacing between children increases
   c. the duration of the breastfeeding period increases
   d. the number of surviving children per mother decreases slightly

8. Which of the following is NOT a consequence of domestication?
   a. decline in quality of diet
   b. decrease in labor
   c. reliance on smaller number of plants
   d. environmental degradation

9. Monocropping is the process of _____.
   a. growing one crop per year
   b. growing one crop per field
   c. developing ownership of land
   d. all of the above

10. Which of the following is an advantage of agriculture?
    a. extraction of great amounts of energy
    b. reduction in disease
    c. a predictable food supply
    d. both a and c

Arguing Anthropology

Questions for Discussion and Thought:

1. Was agriculture really "the worst mistake in the history of the human race"?

2. What are the drawbacks of a foraging way of life?

ANSWER KEY

Key Terms Review

1. sedentism
2. Domestication
3. agriculture
4. Natufian tradition
5. broad spectrum foraging
6. Social stratification
7. chiefdom
8. Neolithic
9. monocropping

Multiple Choice Questions

1. c
2. d
3. b
4. b
5. c
6. a
7. a
8. b
9. b
10. d

Chapter 10: The Evolution of Complex Societies

STUDY STRATEGY: USING THE SUMMARY AS A STUDY GUIDE

This textbook contains a lengthy summary for each chapter. These summaries are especially helpful because they include the main ideas and many details. Reading the summary before reading the chapter gives you an outline of the main concepts in the chapter. After reading the chapter, complete the questions in this Study Guide to receive feedback on how well you understood the chapter.

In addition to using the Study Guide, you should think of other questions your instructor could ask. For example, construct your own list of questions from each numbered point in the summary. Since the numbered information in the summary follows in order the information discussed in each section, you can easily find the complete discussion in the chapter. Asking broad questions is a good way to study from the summary. Consider the following questions:

1. Describe foraging societies. How did these societies differ from later societies?
2. How did social stratification develop? What made it possible? What was its effect?
3. What arguments can be presented to prove that "simple" societies were not simple?
4. What archaeological evidence is there to describe a complex society? In what way did the complex society use this evidence?
5. Explain in detail how archaeologists gather information on a complex society.
6. How do archaeologists classify (categorize) societies? What evidence do they use to classify the societies? How do civilization and cultural creativity go together? (In the section Archaeological Evidence for Social Complexity, the text includes a chart, listing each category—band, tribe, chiefdom, state, and empire—and giving a definition.)
7. Explain the problems of using pottery or writing to classify societies at different levels of cultural evolution.
8. Discuss the hypotheses set forth to explain how and why complex societies developed. What are the positive and negative aspects of the hypotheses?
9. Make a timeline of dates (a chart) listing what happened for each time period in Mesopotamia as complex society evolved.

Timeline	What Happened?
9000 years ago	
7500 years ago	
6500 years ago	
6000 years ago	
5600 years ago	
5200 years ago	

10. What are the proposed reasons for the beginning of Mesopotamian city-states?
11. Describe the physical sites where Andean civilization developed. Then make a timeline (a chart) of the events and tell what happened in each time period (see example above).
12. Why can't we determine the distinct causes for the rise of complex societies in the Andes? What are some possible causes?

When studying, read your question, cover the answer in the summary, and recite your answer out loud. If you are tired and are experiencing problems concentrating, write out the answer. Many students "fool" themselves by reciting a few facts and then thinking they know the rest of the information; however, if you can't put the information on paper, you don't know it! In addition, many students are more comfortable learning and remembering information if they use more than one sense. See, recite, listen to yourself, write.

EXERCISES

Key Terms Review

Use the appropriate key term(s) in each sentence that follows.

band	egalitarian societies	social stratification
burials	empire	stamp seals; cylinder seals
chiefdom	monumental architecture	state
civilization	occupational specialization	surplus production
concentrations of particular	rank society	tribe
artifacts	social class	vertical archipelago system
cultural horizon	social complexity	

1. Societies in which no great differences in wealth, power, or prestige divide members from one another are called _____.

2. _____ is a form of social organization in which people have unequal access to wealth, power, and prestige.

3. _____ is a term used to describe societies with large populations, an extensive division of labor, and occupational specialization.

4. The production of amounts of food that exceed the basic subsistence needs of the population is called _____.

5. The specialization in various occupations (such as weaving or pot making) or in new social roles (such as king or priest) that is found in socially complex societies is called _____.

6. A _____ is a sharply distinct category of people defined in terms of wealth, occupation, or other cultural criteria.

7. _____ are those constructions of a greater-than-human scale, such as pyramids, temples, or tombs.

8. _____ are the complex of archaeological features associated with the internment of bodies, such as the presence or absence of objects placed in a grave, the presence and size of grave markers, the structures surrounding a grave site, and so on.

9. _____ comprise sets of artifacts indicating that particular social activities took place at a particular area in an archaeological site when that site was inhabited in the past.

10. In a _____, the characteristic form of social organization found among foragers, a small group of people, usually with 50 or fewer members, divide labor according to age and sex, and keep social relations that are highly egalitarian.

11. A form of social organization generally larger than a band is a _____; members usually farm or herd for a living. Social relations are relatively egalitarian, although there may be a "chief" who speaks for the group or organizes certain group activities.

12. _____ is a term used by some anthropologists in preference to "tribe" to describe a society that is relatively egalitarian but may have a "chief" who is often accorded greater prestige but ordinarily has no greater power or wealth than other members of the society.

13. A _____ is a form of social organization in which the leader and his close relatives are set apart from the rest of the society and allowed privileged access to wealth, power, and prestige.

14. A _____ is a stratified society that possesses a territory that is defended from outside enemies by an army and from internal disorder by police. It has a separate set of governmental institutions designed to enforce laws and to collect taxes and tribute, and it is run by an elite who possesses a monopoly on the use of force.

15. A(n) _____ is a political network created when one state conquers neighboring states.

16. A widespread uniformity in material culture that appears suddenly in the archaeological record is called a _____.

17. For archaeologists, a _____ is the flowering of cultural creativity that accompanies the rise of state societies and persists for a long time.

18. Tools made in early complex southwestern Asian societies in order to impress distinctive images in clay

    are called _____ or _____.

19. The _____ is a distinctive Andean pattern of integrating economic resources

    from a variety of environments between the highlands and the coast, thus providing the society in

    general with a full range of products from each zone.

Multiple Choice Questions

1. Which of the following areas did NOT give rise to one of the first states?
    a. Andes
    b. Egypt
    c. central Europe
    d. Indus Valley

2. What makes a complex society complex?
    a. social organization
    b. increased intelligence in the population
    c. knowledge of the natural environment
    d. all of the above

3. Which of the following is NOT a form of monumental architecture?
    a. a pyramid
    b. a royal tomb
    c. a farm house
    d. a temple

4. A stratified society with a leader and his close relatives given privileged access to wealth, power, and
    prestige is called a _____.
    a. band
    b. chiefdom
    c. state
    d. tribe

5. Monumental public buildings, highly developed crafts, and regional settlement patterns with at least
    three levels of social complexity are archaeological indicators of a _____.
    a. band
    b. chiefdom
    c. state
    d. tribe

6. Which of the following ancient civilizations had no writing system?
    a. Aztec
    b. Egyptian
    c. Inca
    d. Sumerian

7. Carneiro's theory of the rise of the first states is based on _____.
   a. warfare
   b. population pressure
   c. fertile land surrounded by infertile environments
   d. all of the above

8. Which of the following have NOT been used to explain the rise of civilizations?
   a. technological factors
   b. economic factors
   c. sociocultural factors
   d. all have been used as explanations

9. In Mesopotamia, the first states appeared about _____.
   a. 10,000 years ago
   b. 7,500 years ago
   c. 5,000 years ago
   d. 2,500 years ago

10. The distinctive Andean pattern of integrating economic resources from a variety of environments is called _____.
    a. environmental circumscription
    b. peninsular farming system
    c. state-sponsored feasting system
    d. vertical archipelago system

Arguing Anthropology

Questions for discussion and thought:

1. To what degree are inequality and violence a fundamental part of the social system of the state?

2. The reasons for the emergence of the state as a form of social organization are still not clear. What do you think prompted this change in human social organization?

ANSWER KEY

Key Terms Review

1. egalitarian societies
2. Social stratification
3. Social complexity
4. surplus production
5. occupational specialization
6. social class
7. Monumental architecture
8. Burials
9. Concentrations of particular artifacts
10. band
11. tribe
12. Rank society
13. chiefdom
14. state
15. empire
16. cultural horizon
17. civilization
18. stamp seals; cylinder seals
19. vertical archipelago system

Multiple Choice Questions

1. c
2. a
3. c
4. b
5. c
6. c
7. d
8. d
9. c
10. d

Chapter 11: Culture and the Human Condition

STUDY STRATEGY: READING AND REMEMBERING INFORMATION

In the first and second chapters of this Study Guide, the Preview/Read/Review method of reading was discussed. Let's review that method for this chapter.

Previewing

Preview this chapter, Culture and the Human Condition, to learn the structure (outline) of information. Also, look at the pictures and graphs and read the captions. Think about your prior knowledge of this information.

> **Outline: Culture and the Human Condition**
>
> **The Human Condition and Culture**
> **Holism**
> **Cultural Differences**
>   Ethnocentrism
>   The Cross-Cultural Relationship
>   Cultural Relativism
> **Culture, History, and Human Agency**
> **The Promise of the Anthropological Perspective**
> **Key Terms**
> **Chapter Summary**

Reading

Try to schedule your reading before going to class so you will have an easier time understanding the lecture and taking notes. Before reading each section, think about what you already know. For example, before beginning to read the section entitled The Human Condition and Culture, ask yourself: What do I know about the human condition, human nature? As you read, ask questions: Is this what I know? What new ideas are the authors telling me? After reading the section, stop and answer your questions.

The authors of this textbook help you, the reader, by asking questions and then answering them. For example, the authors begin the first section, The Human Condition and Culture, with two questions: "What is the world like? And what is the human condition within the world?" As you continue through the chapter, read the headings, and think about what you know. After completing the section, stop and recite your answers. Underline, highlight, or take notes as you read.

Authors sometimes also use unique writing patterns to help you understand a concept. Go to the beginning of this chapter and look at the way the opening of the chapter is organized. The first paragraph discusses characteristics of humans and ends with the statement that culture is learned. In the next three paragraphs, the authors continue to discuss how culture is learned and shared, and introduce the adaptive component of culture. Paragraph five adds, "Finally, culture is symbolic." In the sixth and final paragraph, the authors restate the four components and summarize the concepts presented in this section on culture.

Reviewing

Go back and review your notes and parts you underlined. As you review, relate information to the major heading for the section. For example, the section on cultural differences has three parts: Ethnocentrism, The Cross-Cultural Relationship, and Cultural Relativism. As you review the three parts, consider the way they relate to the heading, Cultural Differences.

For the vocabulary you did not know, decide to either write the page number, meaning, and an example in your textbook, or write this information on note cards. Review the information often to keep the ideas fresh in your memory.

EXERCISES

Key Terms Review

Use the appropriate key term(s) in each sentence that follows.

cultural relativism   holism
culture   idealism
determinism   materialism
dialectical relationship   reductionism
dualism   symbol
ethnocentrism

1. _____ may be defined as sets of learned behavior and ideas that human beings acquire as members of society. Human beings use culture both to adapt to and to transform the world in which we live.

2. A _____ is something that stands for something else, and signals the presence of an important domain of experience.

3. _____ is the philosophical view that reality consists of two equal and irreducible forces.

4. The philosophical view called _____ (dating back at least as far as Plato) holds that ideas—or the mind that produces such ideas—constitute the essence of human nature.

5. The philosophical view that the material activities of our physical bodies in the material world constitute the essence of human nature is known as _____.

6. _____ is the philosophical view that explains all evidence in terms of a single set of explanatory principles.

7. The philosophical view that one simple force (or a few simple forces) causes complex events is called _____.

8. _____ is a perspective on the human condition that assumes that mind and body, individuals and society, and individuals and the environment interpenetrate and even define one another.

9. A _____ is a network of cause and effect in which the various causes and effects affect each other.

10. The opinion that one's own way of life is natural or correct, and, indeed, is the only true way of being fully human, is called _____.

11. _____ consists of understanding another culture in its own terms sympathetically enough so that the culture appears to be a coherent and meaningful design for living.

Multiple Choice Questions

1. Which of the following is NOT part of the anthropological definition of culture?
   a. adaptive
   b. innate
   c. shared
   d. symbolic

2. The position called dualism holds that _____.
   a. reality is made up of two radically different elements, mind and matter
   b. matter is the essence of the universe and mind is developed out of it
   c. mind and matter interpenetrate each other
   d. the whole is greater than the sum of its parts

3. Idealism:materialism::
   a. thought:action
   b. dualism:holism
   c. mind:matter
   d. human beings:natural environment

4. A network of cause and effect in which the various causes and effects affect each other is called _____.
   a. dualism
   b. a dialectical relationship
   c. holism
   d. reductionism

5. Ethnocentrism is a form of _____.
   a. scientific research
   b. refusing to make judgements
   c. reductionism
   d. all of the above

6. If we take culture seriously, then the truth in any cultural tradition must be _____.
    a. partial
    b. approximate
    c. open to growth
    d. all of the above

7. The goal of cultural relativism is _____.
    a. change
    b. coexistence
    c. judgment
    d. understanding

8. Which of the following is true of cultural relativism?
    a. It requires us to abandon every value our own culture has taught us.
    b. It makes it possible for us to prove the way a people's culture makes them do things whether they like it or not.
    c. It requires us to take into account many things before we make up our minds.
    d. It frees us from having to face choices between alternatives whose "rightness" and "wrongness" is less than clear-cut.

9. When human beings exercise some control over their own behavior, they are said to be _____.
    a. active
    b. agents
    c. ethnocentric
    d. free

10. The environments in which human beings live are _____.
    a. complex
    b. fluctuating
    c. ambiguous
    d. all of the above

Arguing Anthropology

Questions for discussion and thought:

1. At the time this question is being written, Hutus and Tutsi are slaughtering each other in Rwanda. Can cultural relativism help explain why this is happening and why the French have sent military forces to that country?

2. What is the human condition in the world? What does it mean to be a human being?

ANSWER KEY

Key Terms Review

1. Culture
2. symbol
3. Dualism
4. idealism
5. materialism
6. Reductionism
7. determinism
8. Holism
9. dialectical relationship
10. ethnocentrism
11. Cultural relativism

Multiple Choice Questions

1. b
2. a
3. c
4. b
5. c
6. d
7. d
8. c
9. b
10. d

Chapter 12: Ethnographic Fieldwork

STUDY STRATEGY: MIDBOOK EVALUATION OF STUDY STRATEGIES

You should do a midterm evaluation to determine

- what your grades are at midterm,
- what you must still do for your classes,
- how much background knowledge you have of the information,
- what strategies are effective for you, and
- what changes you plan to make so you will meet your goals of learning the information and passing the classes with the grades you want.

Because the factors of attitude and motivation may have an impact on your achievement, you should also consider your attitude toward your classes and your motivation to study. Since you are at the midpoint of this textbook, it is an appropriate time for you to plan what you will do for the rest of this course.

Midbook Evaluation	
1. What is your grade now? What grade do you want?	
2. What do you still have to do? • *Textbook:* How much do you have to read for the next test? • *Lecture notes:* Do you have a good set of notes? Missing notes? Vague notes? • *Papers/Projects:* What do you have to do?	
3. What type of test(s) will you have? • *Multiple choice?* Fact questions? Application questions? • *Essay test?*	
4. How much background knowledge do you have of information in the rest of this book?	
5. What strategies are effective for you? • *Reading your textbook:* Using the Preview/Read/Review method? Asking numerous questions to test your knowledge?	

• *Note-taking:* Cross-checking your notes with classmates? Reviewing & reciting often? • *Charting & mapping:* Would organizing information into a chart or map help? • *Notecards:* Would writing vocabulary cards help? • *Group study:* Have a friend or friends to study with? • *Instructor and tutors:* Getting extra help with your questions? • *Tests:* Predicting test questions? If you have an essay test, are you writing out answers to practice and determine if you know the information? • *Procrastination:* Are you avoiding the procrastination virus? Allowing adequate time to read and learn the information?	
6. What additional strategies would help you?	
7. What is your attitude? Positive? Negative? Overwhelmed? How can you make life more comfortable for yourself?	
8. What can you do to motivate yourself to study?	

In summary, students who are effective learners analyze what they know and must do, decide upon the study strategies that will fit the situation, monitor their comprehension and retention (Am I understanding? Am I remembering?), and modify or change their strategies as needed. So, how are you doing? What is your plan for the rest of this anthropology course?

EXERCISES

Key Terms Review

Use the appropriate key term(s) in each sentence that follows.

culture shock   objective knowledge
facts   participant-observation
fieldwork   positivism
informant   reflexivity
interpretation   translation
intersubjective meanings

1. _____ is the extended period of close involvement with the people in whose language or way of life anthropologists are interested, during which anthropologists collect most of their data.

2. The feeling, akin to panic, that develops in people living in an unfamiliar society when they cannot understand what is happening around them is known as _____.

3. The method anthropologists use to gather information by living as closely as possible to the people whose culture they are studying while participating in their lives as much as possible is known as _____.

4. _____ is the view that there is a reality "out there" that can be known through the senses and that there is a single, appropriate set of scientific methods for investigating that reality.

5. _____ knowledge is knowledge about reality that is absolute and true.

6. People in a particular culture, known as _____, work with anthropologists and provide them with insights about their way of life.

7. _____ refers to the shared public symbolic systems of a culture.

8. _____ can be defined as critically thinking about the way one thinks or reflecting on one's own experience.

9. The process of "bringing to understanding" is called _____.

10. In anthropological fieldwork, the term _____ refers to the process of learning one culture in terms that can be explained to members of another culture.

11. In anthropology, _____ are created and recreated (1) in the field, (2) when the fieldworker, back home, reexamines field notes and is transported back into the field experience, and (3) when the fieldworker discusses his or her experiences with other anthropologists.

Multiple Choice Questions

1. The anthropological research method that relies primarily on face-to-face contact with people as they go about their daily lives is called _____.
   a. controlled comparison
   b. interviewing
   c. scientific observation
   d. participant-observation

2. The research position whose goal is objective knowledge is called _____.
   a. cultural anthropology
   b. interpretivism
   b. positivism
   c. reflexivity

3. Field methods and knowledge in cultural anthropology are closely connected because _____.
   a. one person is studying other people
   b. objectivity is impossible
   c. anthropology is a holistic discipline
   d. anthropologists pay attention to certain kinds of information but not other kinds

4. Which of the following sentences describes the kinds of people who tend to become an anthropologist's key informants?
   a. They are able to give external form to their own experiences by presenting them to meet the anthropologist's questions.
   b. They tend to be rather marginal in their own societies.
   c. They have the ability to explain even the most obvious things to a foreigner in a variety of ways.
   d. all of the above

5. Reflexivity is _____.
   a. an automatic response
   b. thinking about thinking
   c. the outcome of objective observation and dispassionate analysis
   d. a key principle of positivist science

6. What kinds of responsibilities do anthropologists have to the people with whom they work?
   a. to never disagree with them in public
   b. to protect their identities if necessary
   c. to speak for them since they are unable to do so
   d. to represent them in national courts

7. Why did the Quichua-speakers of Otavalo, Ecuador, invite the anthropologist Lawrence Carpenter to drink chicha with them?
   a. They had accepted him as a part of the group.
   b. They wanted him to experience their traditional feasting.
   c. They wanted to test him.
   d. They felt that he would be able to learn more of their language by drinking with them.

8. Meaning in culture is _____.
   a. always assured
   b. constructed by those who use it
   c. the product of those who know the culture best
   d. something which needs to be discovered by careful participant-observation

9. When Jean Briggs spoke in anger to the white sportsmen, her Utku family _____.
   a. praised her and made her feel that she was really one of them
   b. were quietly respectful of her willingness to defend them
   c. punished her by isolating her
   d. expelled her from the village after an angry argument

10. The facts of anthropology _____.
   a. speak for themselves
   b. are created by anthropologists working with their informants
   c. are fundamentally a matter of opinion
   d. are part of the objective social reality that the anthropologist tries to discover

Arguing Anthropology

Questions for discussion and thought:

1. What is the value of culture shock?

2. If the facts of cultural anthropology are "constructed," does cultural anthropology become just one person's opinion?

ANSWER KEY

Key Terms Review

1. Fieldwork
2. culture shock
3. participant-observation
4. Positivism
5. Objective
6. informants
7. Intersubjective meaning
8. Reflexivity
9. interpretation
10. translation
11. facts

Multiple Choice Questions

1. d
2. b
3. a
4. d
5. b
6. b
7. c
8. b
9. c
10. b

Chapter 13: History, Anthropology, and the Explanation of Cultural Diversity

STUDY STRATEGY: MEMORY: VISUALIZING INFORMATION II

In Chapter 9, we discussed several study strategies to help you visualize information so you could enhance your ability to understand and recall information. Let's review those ideas.

Strategies to Help Comprehension and Recall

1. Drawing pictures.
    Do you ever wish the authors had included a picture or illustration so the information would be clearer to you? See if you can draw a picture of what is happening.

2. Making visual images.
    When reading novels or short stories, it is usually easy to visualize what is happening. In the same manner, it is usually easy to visualize what is happening in the stories the authors use at the beginning of each chapter. Although it is not as easy to use visualization in other parts of this textbook, you can try to use the technique in some parts. Visualization may help comprehension because you have to focus attention on the information, and the mental images may help you make the information more concrete, more real.

    Let's try to use visualization with information from the section The Effects of Western Expansion. In the subsection Background and History, the text gives a timeline of European exploration. When you read this section, make a mental map of the countries of Holland, England, France, Portugal, Spain, Egypt, and the continent of Africa (especially the coastline going around Cape of Good Hope). If you can't picture the area, get a map and locate the area so you can make the information more real instead of just words on a page. Think about what happened; that is, what the explorers did and why.

    In the next subsection, Effects of Expansion in Africa and the Americas, the text discusses how, at first, explorers were only able to work with the people on the coastline of Africa. Make a mental map of Africa and know why the explorers were restricted to the coastline and what the effects were of this arrangement. Next, the text discusses the arrival of European explorers in the Americas. Make a mental map of the Americas. Compare and contrast what happened in Africa with what happened in the Americas. With some paragraphs you can easily visualize what happened because of the vivid description. For example:

    > Indigenous American societies disrupted by disease and conquest suffered further dislocation after Spanish colonial administration was established. The government in Spain was determined to control the exploitation of the new territories. It strove to check the attempts of colonists to set themselves up as feudal lords commanding local Native American groups as their peasants. These efforts were far from successful. Conquered Native Americans were put to work in mines and on plantations. Hard labor further reduced their numbers and fractured their traditional forms of social organization. By the time the worst of these abuses were finally curtailed, in the early seventeenth century, the nature of Native American society in New Spain had been drastically reshaped.

3. Using charts to visualize information.

A previous chapter discussed the study strategy of organizing information into charts. The text also uses a chart in Figure 13.1 to depict the sequence of ethnical periods suggested by Morgan. If it is possible, some students prefer to summarize information in a chart instead of writing out the information in a paragraph because seeing how the information is categorized helps them understand it more easily. When reviewing, they can visualize their chart easier than they can visualize their paragraphs.

To summarize, memory may be strengthened by coding information for storage in your mind by using several senses—listen to yourself read, write notes, make charts, and visualize what is happening.

EXERCISES

Key Terms Review

Use the appropriate key term(s) in each sentence that follows.

band	social structure	typology
chiefdom	state	unilineal cultural evolutionism
culture area	structural-functional theory	
culture traits	tribe	

1. A _____ is a classification system based, in this case, on forms of human society.

2. A nineteenth-century theory that proposed a series of stages through which all societies must go (or had gone) in order to reach "civilization" is known as _____

3. The enduring aspects of the social forms in a society, including its political and kinship systems, make up the _____.

4. A _____ is the characteristic form of social organization found among foragers, made up of a small group of people, usually with 50 or fewer members. Labor is divided according to age and sex, and social relations are highly egalitarian.

5. A _____ is a form of social organization generally larger than the band; members usually farm or herd for a living. Social relations are relatively egalitarian, although members may have a leader who speaks for the group, or organizes certain group activities.

6. A _____ is a form of social organization in which the leader and his close relatives are set apart from the rest of the society and allowed privileged access to wealth, power, and prestige.

7. A _____ is a stratified society that possesses territories which it defends from outside enemies with an army and from internal disorder with police. It has a separate set of governmental institutions designed to enforce laws and to collect taxes and tribute and is run by an elite who possesses a monopoly on the use of force.

8. A position that explores how particular social forms function from day to day in order to reproduce the traditional structure of the society is called a _____.

9. Particular features or parts of a cultural tradition, such as a dance or a ritual, are called _____.

10. A _____ marks the limits of borrowing, or the diffusion, of a particular trait or set of traits.

Multiple Choice Questions

1. In the societies they have visited, anthropologists have usually been preceded for many years by explorers, colonial administrators, and missionaries. This illustrates the saying _____.
   a. the informant is always right
   b. people outside the Western world are people without history
   c. might makes right
   d. there is no such thing as pre-contact ethnography

2. European expansion into the rest of the world in the fifteenth and sixteenth centuries was
   a. motivated by commercial interests
   b. accidental
   c. the outcome of competition with China
   d. led by Christian missionaries

3. With regard to the European contact with Africa and the Americas, _____.
   a. disease made the Europeans suffer greatly on both continents, slowing their conquest
   b. Europeans were confined to the African coast for many years, but rapidly conquered deeply into the Americas
   c. slavery proved to be the key for European economic exploitation of the colonies in Africa but not in the Americas
   d. trade with established kingdoms provided the Europeans with exceptional wealth until the mid-nineteenth century

4. Classifications of human societies help us to _____.
   a. see reality in an undistorted way
   b. perceive the sharp boundaries that separate societies from one another
   c. see some of the ways societies are similar and different, while obscuring others
   d. both a and b

5. A theory that holds that all societies pass through a series of stages in order to reach "civilization" is called _____.
   a. structural-functionalism
   b. unilineal cultural evolutionism
   c. diffusionism
   d. social structural

6. Among the practical problems faced by colonial administrators in the late nineteenth and early twentieth centuries was(were) _____.
   a. keeping the peace among the various colonized groups
   b. applying aspects of European law uniformly
   c. eliminating witchcraft
   d. all of the above

7. The enduring aspects of the social forms in a society, including its political and kinship systems, are called _____.
   a. cultural areas
   b. independent inventions
   c. voluntary organizations
   d. social structure

8. The form of research called "cultural area studies" is most associated with _____.
   a. Lewis Henry Morgan
   b. unilineal cultural evolutionists
   c. Franz Boas
   d. structural-functionalists

9. Which of the following factors sets the indigenous peoples of the Northwest Coast of North America apart from other foragers?
   a. They possess no domesticated animals.
   b. They live in large, settled villages.
   c. Their social organization is highly egalitarian.
   d. They eat fish.

10. Anthropologists classify human societies in more than one way because _____.
    a. new data demonstrate that the old classifications are wrong
    b. different anthropologists ask different kinds of questions
    c. anthropologists cannot agree on the importance of political organization versus economic organization
    d. some anthropologists do not do field research and do not have an appropriate basis for classification

Arguing Anthropology

Questions for discussion and thought:

1. How have the contacts between the West and the rest of the world affected the development of anthropology?

2. How do the classifications of societies available at any given moment shape people's political and economic decisions?

ANSWER KEY

Key Terms Review

1. typology
2. unilineal cultural evolutionism
3. social structure
4. band
5. tribe
6. chiefdom
7. state
8. structural-functional theory
9. culture trait
10. culture area

Multiple Choice Questions

1. d
2. a
3. b
4. c
5. b
6. d
7. c
8. c
9. b
10. b

Chapter 14: Language

STUDY STRATEGY: PROBLEMS AND SOLUTIONS

Students encounter a number of problems when studying. Do any of these problems sound familiar to you?

Problem 1: Effective Study Strategies

Do you ever complain that even though you studied, you did not do well on the test? Why did this happen? Have you thought about your learning style? What strategies or techniques help you learn and remember information?

Possible Solutions

Monitor your comprehension and retention of information and decide which of the following strategies would be the most helpful to you:

1. Reading: If you have extensive background knowledge of the concepts discussed in this anthropology book, just reading the information may be enough. However, if much of the information is new to you, try the Preview/Read/Review method discussed in Chapter 1.
2. Notes: Using the main headings as an outline, take notes on the information. Writing the information may help you remember it later.
3. Note Cards: Use note cards for the key terms. Write the term on the front side and the meaning plus an example on the reverse side of the card. Review often.
4. Underlining or Highlighting: As you read, underline or highlight important ideas and details. You could color-code as you underline; for example, underline main ideas in red and the details and examples in another color. One disadvantage to underlining or highlighting is that some students have said they can underline or highlight and sleep at the same time; they dont really concentrate on what they are doing. Another disadvantage is that some students underline or highlight too much. Have you ever purchased a used textbook and found whole pages that are underlined or highlighted? Be selective about the information you underline or highlight. Also, concentrate on the information.
5. Reviewing: Since we tend to forget information rapidly, review often. Beginning to review three days before the test will not allow you adequate time to learn the information. Therefore, decide how often you need to review your notes and the information you have underlined. Students who review often say taking the test is usually more comfortable.
6. Reciting: Cover your notes and recite the information—out loud, if possible. Using more than one avenue of learning may be more effective for you (see, hear, write).
7. Study Groups: Discussing the information with someone else can add to your depth of understanding because you are learning the information from another viewpoint, another perspective. Also, studying with someone else can help motivate you.

To summarize, strategies which include active participation tend to increase your ability to remember, by involving you in the study process. Learning is an active process! So think about your learning style and decide which strategies work best for you.

Problem 2: Procrastination

Do you make plans to read your anthropology assignment, but never get around to doing it? Do you leave yourself so little time to get your reading done that you just skim-read?

Possible Solutions

1. Make a study schedule. The classes you like the least should come first on your schedule. Be realistic; do not underestimate the amount of time you need to read and learn anthropology.
2. Study with a friend. This can add motivation.
3. Set definite, achievable goals; for example, plan to read five pages or write ten vocabulary cards.
4. Give yourself a reward when you have completed your goals. Go for a walk. Watch your favorite television program.

Problem 3: Getting Additional Help

Have you analyzed how you studied and what strategies helped you do well? Are there people who can help you?

Possible Solutions

1. Instructor: See your instructor and discuss the upcoming test. What ideas can your instructor give you concerning learning the information in this book? What ideas does the instructor have for preparing for the test?
2. Tutors: Most colleges and universities have free tutoring services. Ask your instructor if the department provides tutoring. To determine whether your college/university has a Tutoring Center, check the college catalog, or ask a counselor at your Counseling Center.

EXERCISES

Key Terms Review

Use the appropriate key term(s) in each sentence that follows.

cognition
communicative competence
design features
language
linguistic competence
linguistics
metaphor
morphology

phonology
pidgin
pragmatics
prototypes
Sapir-Whorf hypothesis
schema
semantics
syntax

1. _____ is the system of arbitrary vocal symbols we use to encode our experience of the world.

2. The scientific study of language is called _____.

3. Those characteristics of language that, when taken together, differentiate it from other known animal communication systems are called _____.

4. _____ may be defined as (1) the mental process by which human beings gain knowledge; (2) the nexus of relations between the mind at work and the world in which it works.

5. A term coined by linguist Noam Chomsky to refer to the mastery of adult grammar is _____.

6. The term _____, coined by anthropological linguist Dell Hymes, refers to the mastery of adult rules for socially and culturally appropriate speech.

7. The _____ is a position that asserts that language has the power to shape the way people see the world.

8. The study of the sounds of language is _____.

9. In linguistics, _____ is the study of word structure.

10. _____ is the study of sentence structure.

11. _____ refers to the study of meaning.

12. The study of language in the context of its use is known as _____.

13. A _____ refers to patterned, repetitive experiences.

14. _____ are examples of a typical instance, element, relation, or experience within a particular, culturally relevant semantic domain.

15. Aspects of thought that assert a meaningful link between two expressions from different semantic domains are known as _____.

16. A _____ is a language with no native speakers that develops in a single generation between members of communities that possess distinct native languages.

Multiple Choice Questions

1. The transfer of information from one person to another is called _____.
   a. communication
   b. language
   c. speech
   d. phonology

2. With regard to complexity, _____.
   a. some languages are significantly more complex than others in terms of grammar
   b. all languages are equally complex
   c. some languages are more primitive in vocabulary and grammar
   d. linguistic complexity only varies in terms of vocabulary, not in terms of the needs of speakers to express themselves

3. There is nothing inherent in the nature of a large quadruped well-suited for long distance running that requires us to call this creature a "horse." This illustrates the linguistic design feature of _____.
   a. specialization
   b. definition
   c. semanticity
   d. arbitrariness

4. The mastery of adult roles for socially and culturally appropriate speech refers to _____.
   a. cognitive competence
   b. communicative competence
   c. grammatical competence
   d. linguistic competence

5. Linguistic determinism is a view that _____.
   a. culture is a variety of language
   b. grammar is determined by the wider culture
   c. grammar determines how people think about the world
   d. the determinants of language and culture are to be found in the structure of the human mind

6. Which component of language is concerned with the way words are put together?
   a. morphology
   b. phonology
   c. semantics
   d. syntax

7. Separating the various parts of speech into categories that represent the building blocks of the sentence is called _____.
   a. deep structure
   b. grammar
   c. operational definition
   d. structural grouping

8. In the course of conversation, different speakers may represent elements of the same nonlinguistic context differently. That is, each speaker _____.
   a. takes up a different referential perspective with regard to the context
   b. takes up a different ideological perspective with regard to the context
   c. is incapable of escaping the categories of his/her language to learn to see the world in a different way
   d. both a and b

9. In his studies of speech in the inner city, William Labov recognized that, when African American children were interviewed by European American adults in school classrooms, _____.
   a. their responses were defensive attempts to keep threatening questioners from learning anything about them
   b. they said very little
   c. they were unable to produce grammatical utterances
   d. both a and b

10. A form of thought and language that asserts a meaningful link between two expressions from different semantic domains is called _____.
    a. literal language
    b. metaphor
    c. a prototype
    d. a schema

Arguing Anthropology

Questions for discussion and thought:

1. Does language determine thought?

2. Do men and women in the United States "speak the same language?"

ANSWER KEY

Key Terms Review	Multiple Choice Questions

Key Terms Review

1. Language
2. linguistics
3. design features
4. Cognition
5. linguistic competence
6. communicative competence
7. Sapir-Whorf hypothesis
8. phonology
9. morphology
10. Syntax
11. Semantics
12. pragmatics
13. schema
14. Prototypes
15. metaphor
16. pidgin

Multiple Choice Questions

1. a
2. b
3. d
4. b
5. c
6. a
7. d
8. d
9. d
10. b

Chapter 15: Cognition

EXERCISES

Key Terms Review

Use the appropriate key term(s) in each sentence that follows.

articulated style
cognition
cognitive capacities
cognitive style
elementary cognitive processes
emotion
enculturation
functional cognitive systems

global style
logic
perception
rational thinking
reasoning styles
self
socialization
syllogistic reasoning

1. The mental characteristics that enable us to receive signals from the outside world (or from within our own bodies) and to interpret these signals in a way that makes appropriate action possible are called

   _____.

2. _____ consist of the ability to make abstractions, reason inferentially, and categorize.

3. Culturally linked sets of cognitive processes that guide perception, conception, reason, and emotion are called _____.

4. _____ consists of the processes by which people organize and experience information that is primarily of sensory origin.

5. Recurring patterns of cognitive activity that characterize an individual's perceptual and intellectual activities make up his or her _____.

6. _____ is a holistic way of viewing the world. People who use such a style first see a bundle of relationships and only later see the bits and pieces that are related. They are said to be *field dependent*.

7. _____ is a way of viewing the world that breaks it up into smaller and smaller pieces which can then be organized. People who use such a style consider whatever they happen to be paying attention to apart from its context. They are said to be *field independent*.

8. _____ is (1) the mental process by which human beings gain knowledge, and (2) the nexus of relations between the mind at work and the world in which it works.

9. _____ is an active cognitive process that involves going beyond the information given.

10. A form of reasoning based on a series of three statements in which the first two statements are the premises and the last is the conclusion, which must follow from the premises, is known as _____.

11. The way we understand a cognitive task, the way we encode the information presented to us, the transformations that the information undergoes, and the factors that control them make up our _____.

12. _____ is a symbolic system used to represent objects and relationships between objects in the world.

13. _____ is the product of a dialectic between bodily arousal and cognitive interpretation, comprising states, values, and arousals.

14. The process by which human beings as material organisms, living together with other similar organisms, must learn to pattern and adapt their behavior according to the appropriate behavioral rules established by our respective societies is known as _____.

15. _____ is the process by which human beings, as intelligent, reflexive creatures living with each other, must learn to pattern and adapt their ways of thinking and feeling to the ways of thinking and feeling that are considered appropriate in our respective cultures.

16. The result of the process of socialization/enculturation is the _____.

Multiple Choice Questions

1. Cognition is often thought to encompass which three aspects?
   a. illusion, perception, conception
   b. perception, illusion, emotion
   c. perception, paradox, conception
   d. perception, intellect, emotion

2. According to Vygotsky, elementary cognitive processes are organized into _____.
   a. functional cognitive systems
   b. higher-order cognitive processes
   c. cognitive capacities
   d. schemas

3. The tests that were designed to examine how nonliterate South African mine workers interpret two-dimensional line drawings of three-dimensional objects demonstrate that _____.
   a. the mine workers could not perceive in three dimensions
   b. the drawings make sense only when the viewer accepts certain rules for interpreting them
   c. the mine workers could only interpret the drawings after the drawings were explained to them
   d. both a and b

4. A recurring pattern of perceptual and intellectual activity is a(n) _____.
    a. abstraction
    b. cognitive style
    c. prototype
    d. perceptual capacity

5. Kenge, an Mbuti from Zaire, mistook distant buffalo for insects because _____.
    a. they were small buffalo
    b. he was seeing them from an airplane
    c. he had never seen them from such a great distance
    d. in his functional cognitive system, the features of buffalo and insects overlapped

6. When Roy D'Andrade tested UCSD students on syllogistic reasoning, they were less able to complete a syllogism correctly when _____.
    a. the content was arbitrary
    b. it was presented in mathematical form
    c. it was presented on a test, rather than in classroom discussion
    d. all of the above

7. What might have been the evolutionary selective value of emotional responses in humans?
    a. They enable us to be more fully human.
    b. They make us better parents to our offspring.
    c. They alert us to something new and unexpected in our environment.
    d. They allow learning to take place.

8. Catherine Lutz' study of emotion among Ifaluk people demonstrates that _____.
    a. the language of emotion can be a way of talking about social relationships
    b. emotions that appear to be quite distinct from Western emotions are actually quite similar
    c. the internal bodily states registered by the Ifaluk are distinct from those registered by people in other kinds of environments
    d. emotions have more to do with politics than with internal bodily states

9. Which term highlights the ways in which human beings must learn to pattern their ways of thinking and feeling and adapt them to the ways of thinking and feeling considered appropriate in the culture in which they were born?
    a. accommodation
    b. assimilation
    c. enculturation
    d. socialization

10. The zone of proximal development is _____.
    a. the next stage in the socialization process
    b. the distance between a child's actual development level and its potential development level
    c. a way of measuring the cognitive capacities of a child by discovering what the child is unable to do at a given moment
    d. what a child can do itself, compared to what an older child can do

Arguing Anthropology

Questions for discussion and thought:

1. Can cross-cultural relationships (ranging from ethnographic fieldwork to friendship to love and long-term intimate relationships) survive the cultural differences in perception, conception, and especially emotion?

2. If the zone of proximal development is so important in understanding learning, why do many Western people consider it to be a form of cheating?

ANSWER KEY

Key Terms Review

1. cognitive capacities
2. Elementary cognitive processes
3. functional cognitive systems
4. Perception
5. cognitive style
6. Global style
7. Articulated style
8. Cognition
9. Rational thinking
10. syllogistic reasoning
11. reasoning styles
12. Logic
13. Emotion
14. socialization
15. Enculturation
16. self

Multiple Choice Questions

1. d
2. a
3. b
4. b
5. c
6. a
7. c
8. a
9. c
10. b

Chapter 16: Play, Art, Myth, and Ritual

STUDY STRATEGY: **ORGANIZING INFORMATION AND MAKING CONNECTIONS**

A previous chapter discussed strategies that authors and students use to organize information and make connections between ideas. Let's revisit these strategies and add a new one: having a mental conversation with yourself as you read this textbook. Again, the purpose of the strategies is to help you focus attention on the relationship between ideas, so you will have a higher comfort level when learning the information and taking your tests.

Authors: Organizing Information to Help Students Make Connections

Immediately after the story about the heavyweight boxing fight in the introduction to this chapter, the authors include a paragraph in which they ask questions to get you to think about the way we view events. They want you to make connections with your background knowledge about play, art, myth, and ritual, and to use your knowledge as a beginning point for information covered in the chapter.

The last paragraph of the introduction states what will be presented in this chapter, thus connecting the story and your background information to the new information in this chapter.

> In this chapter, we consider how anthropologists go about trying to make sense of events similar to the event in the bar. We will examine play, art, myth, and ritual—four elements of human experience that are related to each other in some interesting and provocative ways. Indeed, their interrelationships are the focus of some of the most exciting work being done in anthropology today.

After the first heading, **Play**, the text makes a connection with the previous chapter by telling you what was discussed in the last chapter and what will be new in this chapter:

> . . . In the previous two chapters, we have explored the concept of openness in linguistic and cognitive settings. Openness was defined as the ability to talk about, or think about, the same thing in different ways and different things in the same way. If we expand openness to include all behavior—that is, the ability not just to talk or think about, but also to do the same thing in different ways or different things in the same way—we begin to define play. All mammals play, and human beings play the most and throughout their lives.

Another way the authors help you make connections is by using signal words ("first," "second," "because," "in addition," "another," "for example," "in contrast"). In the first paragraph after the heading A Definition of Ritual, the authors use signal words so you will easily recognize the four elements of ritual; the signal words have been underlined in this excerpt. After reading the section, you could ask yourself: What are the four elements of ritual? It would be easy to find the four parts because of the signal words:

> Our definition of **ritual** has <u>four</u> elements. <u>First</u>, ritual is a repetitive social practice composed of a sequence of symbolic activities in the form of dance, song, speech, gestures, the manipulations of certain objects, and so forth. <u>Second</u>, it is set off from the social routines of everyday life. <u>Third</u>, rituals in any culture adhere to a characteristic, culturally defined ritual schema. This

means that members of a culture can tell that a certain sequence of activities is a ritual even if they have never seen that particular ritual before. <u>Finally</u>, ritual action is closely connected to a specific set of ideas that are often encoded in myth. These ideas might concern the nature of evil, the relationship of human beings to the spirit world, and so forth. The purpose for which a ritual is performed guides how these ideas are selected and symbolically enacted.

Students: Making Connections through Mental Conversations

Read the following section, Rites of Passage, and notice how the authors divide the rites of passage into three stages. Note the signal words that point out those three stages.

> *Rites of Passage*
>
> Let us examine this process by looking at one kind of ritual performance: the **rite of passage.** At the beginning of the twentieth century, the Belgian anthropologist Arnold Van Gennep noted that certain kinds of rituals around the world had similar structures. These were rituals associated with the movement (or passage) of people from one position in the social structure to another. They included births, initiations, confirmations, weddings, funerals, and the like (1960).
>
> Van Gennep found that all these rituals <u>began with a period</u> of *separation* from the old position and from normal time. During this period, the ritual passenger left behind the symbols and practices of his or her previous position. For example, in induction into military service, recruits leave their families behind and are moved to a new place. They are forced to leave behind the clothing, activities, and even the hair that marked who they were in civilian life.
>
> The <u>second stage</u> in rites of passage involves a period of *transition*, in which the ritual passenger is neither in the old life nor yet in the new one. This period is marked by rolelessness, ambiguity, and perceived danger. It is often a period in which the person or persons involved are subjected to ordeal by those who have already passed through. In military service, this is the period of basic training, in which the recruits (not yet soldiers but no longer civilians) are forced to dress alike and act alike. They are subjected to a grinding-down process, after which they are rebuilt into something new.
>
> During the <u>final stage</u>—*reaggregation*—the ritual passenger is reintroduced into society but in his or her new position. In the military, this involves the graduation from basic training and the visit home, but this time in uniform, on leave, and as a member of the armed forces, a new person.

Monitoring your reading will help you realize whether or not you are recognizing and understanding the relationship, the connection, between ideas. For example, one way to monitor your reading, especially if you are having a difficult time concentrating, is by carrying on a mental conversation. A typical mental conversation might go something like the following:

"Rites of Passage: what are the rites?" "Okay, in a rite of passage we pass from one social position to another, like we're single and then we're married. We live and then we die. I know all the examples, I just didn't call them rites of passage." "'Separation' is a new vocabulary term, and I need to learn it." After beginning the next paragraph, one might say to oneself, "The second stage. Wait a minute! Where is the first stage?" Then one would go back to find the first stage, which is introduced at the beginning of the second paragraph: "Van Gennep found that all these rituals began with a <u>period</u> of *separation* from the old position and from normal time. Okay, that's the first stage." By the fourth paragraph, the reader would mentally comment, "Ok, the final stage. There are three stages in the rites of passage. They are separation from the original role in society, transition into the next role, and reaggregation into the new role."

Do you talk to yourself while you read? Do you sometimes disagree with writers and say, "This is a stupid idea"? Mental conversations can be effective because they help you focus your attention on the ideas and critique what the writer is presenting.

Students: Making Connections by Organizing Information into a Chart

Another way to connect ideas is by taking notes in a chart format. For practice, fill in the information on the following chart:

Stage	Page	What happens?	Examples?
Separation			
Transition			
Reaggrega-tion			

Charting is a learning strategy that requires you to

- generate questions—What are the stages? What happens in each stage? Examples?
- compare and contrast ideas so you recognize the relationship between the stages.
- concentrate on the information.

At this point, you have to add a reciting step to ensure that you will remember the information. Quiz yourself often by asking questions; look away and answer your questions. If you can't concentrate when you are reviewing, write out the information; it's impossible to write and sleep or dream at the same time.

Now let's look at how charting can help with multiple choice and essay questions. Read the following example:

You are a senior, student-teaching in history at a high school. You will graduate in the spring, and plan to begin your teaching career in the fall. At which stage in the rites of passage are you?
a. separation
b. transition
c. reaggregation
d. expert

If you understand the example of the person going into the military service, in the Rites of Passage excerpt given above, you should be able to figure out that a senior who is now a student-teacher has separated from the family, and is in the transitional stage. When the student will be teaching in the fall, the student will be in the reaggregation stage. To the point: in addition to the supporting examples presented by the authors, think of other fitting examples. When doing math problems, students always think of other problems to practice with. When reading books about anthropology or history or psychology, think of other examples. This makes answering application questions easier.

Next let's consider an essay question: "What are rites of passage? Include the stages in your answer." Remember—when writing an essay answer, think of what you want to include (content) and how you want to write it (format, structure). Divide the answer into an introduction, body and summary. Complete the following essay answer.

> Rites of passage are cultural rituals which have common social structures. For example, in a wedding you go from single status to married status; your position in society has changed. The people of the culture recognize that you have "passed" through one stage to another stage. There are three stages in rites of passage: separation, transition, reaggregation.
>
> In the separation stage. . . .
> In the transition stage. . . .
> In the reaggregation stage. . . .
> To summarize. . . .

If you studied your chart, you should be able to complete the body and summary of this answer. The body of the answer includes the definition and examples for the three stages. If your instructor discussed the stages in class and gave additional examples, you could include both the textbook and lecture examples. Better yet, you could discuss your own examples. The summary can be brief. Organizing information into a chart can therefore be effective preparation for essay tests because it allows you to compare and contrast (stages, people, events, theories, governments), and suggests questions to ask about the various categories included.

To summarize, student-generated and author-generated methods of organizing information can help you make connections so you can recognize the relationships between concepts.

EXERCISES

Key Terms Review

Use the appropriate key term(s) in each sentence that follows.

art   metacommunication   reflexivity
communitas   myths   rite of passage
deep play   orthodoxy   ritual
framing   orthopraxy   sport
liminality   play   transformation-representation

1. _____ may be defined as a framing (or orienting context) that is (1) consciously

    adopted by players, (2) somehow pleasurable, and (3) systemically related to what is nonplay by alluding

    to the nonplay world and by transforming the objects, roles, actions, and relations of ends and means

    characteristic of the nonplay world.

2. Communicating about the process of communication itself is called _____.

3. A cognitive boundary that marks certain behaviors as "play" or as "ordinary life" is called

    _____.

4. _____ is critically thinking about the way one thinks; reflecting on one's own

    experience.

5. _____ is a physically exertive activity that is competitive within constraints

    imposed by definitions and rules. It is a component of culture that is ritually patterned and gamelike,

    and consists of varying amounts of play, work, and leisure.

6. Play in which the stakes are so high that, from a utilitarian perspective, it is irrational for anyone to

    engage in it at all is referred to as _____.

7. Play with form producing some aesthetically successful transformation-representation is a way to define

    _____.

8. The process in which experience is transformed as it is represented symbolically in a different medium

    is called _____.

9. _____ are stories whose truth seems self-evident, because they do such a

    good job of integrating our personal experiences with a wider set of assumptions about the way society

    or the world in general, must operate.

10. _____ is "correct doctrine"; the prohibition of deviation from approved mythic

    texts.

11. _____ is a repetitive social practice composed of a sequence of symbolic activities in the form of dance, song, speech, gestures, or the manipulation of objects, adhering to a culturally defined ritual schema, and closely connected to a specific set of ideas that are often encoded in myth.

12. A _____ is a ritual that serves to mark the movement and transformation of an individual from one social position to another.

13. The ambiguous transitional state in a rite of passage in which the persons undergoing the ritual are outside their ordinary social positions is known as _____.

14. _____ is an unstructured or minimally structured community of equal individuals, found frequently in rites of passage.

15. The term _____ refers to "correct practice": the prohibition of deviation from approved forms of ritual behavior.

Multiple Choice Questions

1. If openness is expanded to include all behavior, we begin to define _____.
   a. art
   b. myth
   c. play
   d. ritual

2. What does it mean to say that in play the relationship of means to ends is altered?
   a. Activities or utterances that usually lead to one outcome lead to a different outcome.
   b. The way in which an activity or utterance is carried out changes.
   c. The purpose of an activity or utterance changes.
   d. both a and c

3. Play in which the stakes are so high that, from a utilitarian perspective, it is irrational for anyone to engage in it at all is called _____.
   a. sport
   b. game
   c. deep play
   d. ritual

4. In Brazil, as in many other parts of the world, sport unites people in a common goal, but at the same time often separates _____.
   a. fans and players
   b. mind and body
   c. men and women
   d. upper and lower class people

5. Art is like play, but unlike free play it involves _____.
    a. expressing human standards of beauty
    b. rules for evaluating the form the art takes
    c. expressing human standards of truth
    d. changing the relationship of means to ends

6. In many nonliterate societies, artists _____.
    a. are divorced from the ebb and flow of everyday life
    b. present and represent the basic metaphors of their culture
    c. are concerned with innovation in cultural creation
    d. are frequently found in leadership roles

7. When the Fang evaluated their sculpture for James Fernandez, which of the following factors was NOT of concern to them?
    a. the finished or unfinished quality of the object
    b. whether the quadrants of the work were balanced with one another
    c. whether the proportions of the statue resembled the proportions of living people
    d. whether the statue kept opposites in balance

8. To say that myths have implications for action means that they may _____.
    a. justify past action
    b. explain present action
    c. generate future action
    d. all of the above

9. The idea that myth is a conceptual tool is associated with the work of _____.
    a. Bruce Kapferer
    b. Claude Lévi-Strauss
    c. Bronislaw Malinowski
    d. Victor Turner

10. Which of the following is NOT a part of the definition of ritual?
    a. a repetitive social practice
    b. set off from the social routines of everyday life
    c. created as needed by religious leaders
    d. closely connected to a set of ideas often encoded in myth

11. Which of the following are the stages of a rite of passage?
    a. separation, transformation, readjustment
    b. separation, transition, reaggregation
    c. removal, renovation, reaggregation
    d. communitas, liminality, marginality

Arguing Anthropology

Questions for discussion and thought:

1. What is the attraction of deep play?

2. Victor Turner suggested that communitas was as important as structure. Do you agree?

ANSWER KEY

Key Terms Review

1. Play
2. metacommunication
3. framing
4. Reflexivity
5. Sport
6. deep play
7. art
8. transformation-representation
9. Myths
10. Orthodoxy
11. Ritual
12. rite of passage
13. liminality
14. Communitas
15. orthopraxy

Multiple Choice Questions

1. c
2. d
3. c
4. c
5. b
6. b
7. c
8. d
9. b
10. c
11. b

Chapter 17: Worldview

EXERCISES

Key Terms Review

Use the appropriate key term(s) in each sentence that follows.

computer metaphors
key metaphors
magic
metaphorical entailments
metaphorical predicate
metaphorical subject
metaphors

metonymy
oracles
organic metaphors
priest
religion
revitalization
shaman

societal metaphor
symbol
syncretism
technological metaphors
witchcraft
worldviews

1. _____ are encompassing pictures of reality created by the members of cultures.

2. Aspects of thought that assert a meaningful link between two expressions from different semantic domains are known as _____.

3. The first part of a metaphor, which indicates the domain of experience that needs to be clarified, is the

   _____.

4. The second part of a metaphor, which suggests a familiar domain of experience that may clarify the metaphorical subject, is the _____.

5. _____ are all the attributes of a metaphorical predicate that relate it to the culturally defined domain of experience to which it belongs.

6. The culturally defined relationship of the parts of a semantic domain to the domain as a whole and of the whole to its parts is known as _____.

7. A _____ is something that stands for something else, and signals the presence of an important domain of experience.

8. The performance of evil by human beings believed to possess a nonhuman power to do evil, whether or not it is intentional or self-aware, is known as _____.

9. _____ is a set of beliefs and practices designed to control the visible or invisible world for specific purposes.

10. _____ are invisible forces to which people address questions and whose responses the people believe to be truthful.

11. _____ serve as the foundation of a worldview.

12. The worldview metaphor whose model for the world is the social order is the _____.

13. A worldview metaphor that applies the image of the body to social structures and institutions is called the _____.

14. A worldview metaphor that employs objects made by human beings as metaphorical predicates is known as the _____.

15. A worldview metaphor that employs computers as metaphorical predicates is called the _____.

16. _____ is a worldview in which cosmic forces are personified and dealt with as if they were powerful human beings.

17. A _____ is an individual part-time religious practitioner who is believed to have the power to travel to and/or contact supernatural forces directly on behalf of individuals or groups.

18. A _____ is a religious practitioner skilled in the practice of religious rituals, which he or she carries out for the benefit of the group.

19. The synthesis of a traditional way of life and a new way of life that has been introduced by a different and usually more powerful culture is known as _____.

20. A conscious, deliberate, and organized attempt by some members of a society to create a more satisfying culture is called _____.

Multiple Choice Questions

1. Worldviews aim to encompass _____.
   a. knowledge about the physical universe
   b. the widest understanding of how the world works
   c. a metaphor that everyone understands
   d. the reason people think and feel the way they do

2. In the phrase "He who lives by the sword dies by the sword," the word "sword" is a _____, representing the domain of violence.
   a. metonym
   b. metaphor
   c. simile
   d. none of the above

3. For some citizens of the United States in the summer of 1994, the United States' soccer team, which played in the World Cup tournament, was a(n) _____.
   a. elaborating symbol
   b. oracle
   c. technological metaphor
   d. summarizing symbol

4. The Azande believe that witches get their witchcraft from _____.
   a. their parents
   b. evil thoughts
   c. a supernatural being
   d. training by another witch

5. "We live in a sick society, one that is ravaged by the cancers of crime and drug addiction." This is an example of a(n) _____.
   a. computer metaphor
   b. organic metaphor
   c. societal metaphor
   d. technological metaphor

6. When can metaphors, or the symbols that represent them, be used as instruments of power?
   a. When they are under the direct control of a person wishing to affect the behavior of others.
   b. When they are used for reference or in support of certain conduct.
   c. When some people are able to impose their metaphors on others.
   d. all of the above

7. According to A. F. C. Wallace, there are four major kinds of physiological exercise that induce an ecstatic spiritual state. Which of the following is NOT one of them?
   a. taking drugs
   b. sensory deprivation
   c. eating
   d. mortification of the flesh

8. Priest:Shaman::
   a. collective:individual
   b. indirect:direct
   c. this world:the other world
   d. all of the above

9. A conscious, deliberate, and organized attempt to create a more satisfying culture is called _____.
   a. conversion
   b. resistance
   c. revitalization
   d. syncretism

10. The Bwiti religion of the Fang represents _____.
    a. a response to colonialism and its pressures
    b. an attempt to become Christian in African terms
    c. a way of rejecting everything brought by the colonizers
    d. an attempt to attract wealth from the supernatural world

Arguing Anthropology

Questions for discussion and thought:

1. What makes a worldview compelling?

2. In one of the In Their Own Words selections in this chapter, Andrea Smith writes, "When everyone becomes 'Indian,' then it is easy to lose sight of the specificity of oppression faced by those who are Indian in *this* life. It is no wonder we have such a difficult time finding non-Indians to support our struggles when the New Age movement has completely disguised our oppression." What does she mean? Do you agree?

ANSWER KEY

Key Terms Review

1. Worldviews
2. metaphors
3. metaphorical subject
4. metaphorical predicate
5. Metaphorical entailments
6. metonymy
7. symbol
8. witchcraft
9. Magic
10. Oracles
11. Key metaphors
12. societal metaphor
13. organic metaphor
14. technological metaphor
15. computer metaphor
16. Religion
17. shaman
18. priest
19. syncretism
20. revitalization

Multiple Choice Questions

1. b
2. a
3. d
4. c
5. b
6. d
7. c
8. d
9. c
10. a

Chapter 18: Kinship

STUDY STRATEGY: **GRAPHIC ORGANIZERS**

Charting and mapping information are two forms of graphic organizers that help you focus on the relationship, the connection, between ideas.

Organizing Information into a Chart

Charting was discussed in previous chapters. Let's take a look at another example of charting, from the section Patterns of Descent in Kinship. This section defines and discusses types of descent. The second paragraph begins by saying, "Two major strategies are employed in establishing patterns of descent." The signal word "two" clues you to look for "first" and "second" (or "one," "two"), and this information can be charted. Complete the missing information in the following chart. When studying for your test, ask questions: What are the types of descent? What is the definition of each type? What are examples of each type? How does bilateral descent contrast with unilineal descent?

Descent Type	Page	Definition	Example
Bilateral			
Bilateral descent group			
Bilateral kindred			
Unilineal			
Patrilineal			
Matrilineal			

The information in the section Patterns of Kinship Terminology can also be organized into a chart. Complete the missing information in the chart that follows. Again, when studying for your test, ask yourself questions: What are bilateral kinship patterns? What are unilineal kinship patterns? Describe/define each pattern and give an example. How do the patterns differ from each other?

Kinship Patern	Page	Definition	Example
Bilateral			
Hawaiian			
Eskimo			
Unilineal			
Iroquois			
Crow			
Omaha			
Sudanese			

Organizing Information into a Map

The purpose of the mapping strategy is to show the connection between ideas through the use of a diagram. For example, in this chapter, tree diagrams depict kinship relationships. You can also map (diagram) smaller units of information. For example, in the Kinship and Alliance through Marriage section, the following paragraph appears:

> Anthropologists find two major types of prescriptive marriage patterns in unilineal societies. One is a man's marriage with the "father's sister's daughter." The more common is a man's marriage with the "mother's brother's daughter."

"Father's sister's daughter" and "mother's brother's daughter" can be confusing phrases. Using a diagram to depict the kinship connections can make the phrases easier to understand.

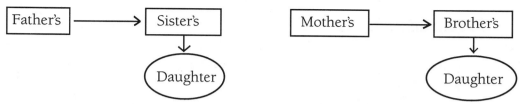

You can also map the main headings and subheadings of a chapter so you can see the relationship, the connection, between the main ideas. Some students color code the levels of information; for example, they might use blue for the topic (Kinship), red for the main headings (Kinship Systems: Ways of Organizing Human Interdependence, or Lineages), and another color for the subheadings (Patrilineages, Matrilineages). Use the headings as questions when studying for a test: What are lineages? How do patrilineages differ from matrilineages?

Following is a sample diagram, representing half of this chapter:

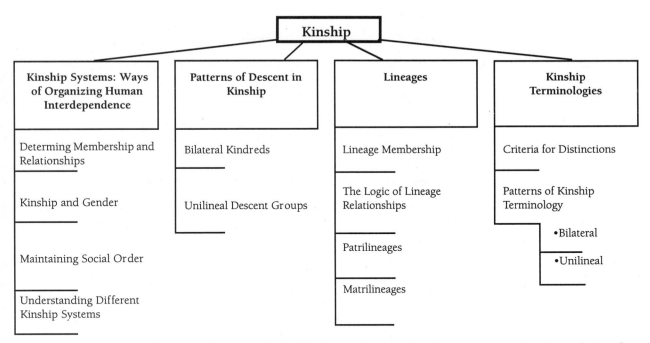

In summary, graphic organizers such as charting and mapping help you perceive the relationship between ideas.

EXERCISES

Key Terms Review

Use the appropriate key term(s) in each sentence that follows.

affinity	*compadrazgo*	marriage
asymmetrical exchange marriage	consanguineal	matrilineage
bifurcation	cross cousins	parallel cousins
bilateral kindred	descent	patrilineage
bilateral descent	direct exchange marriage	segmentary opposition
bridewealth	gender	sex
clan	kinship	unilineal descent
collaterality	lineage	

1. _____ may be defined as social relationships that are prototypically derived from the universal human experiences of mating and birth.

2. _____ is an institution that prototypically involves a man and a woman, transforms the status of the participants, carries implications about permitted sexual access, gives the offspring a position in the society, and establishes connections between the kin of the husband and the kin of the wife.

3. The principle of _____ is based on culturally recognized parent-child connections that define the social categories to which people belong.

4. The observable physical characteristics that distinguish two kinds of human beings, females and males, needed for human biological reproduction are grouped under the umbrella term _____.

5. _____ is the cultural construction of beliefs and behaviors considered appropriate for each sex.

6. _____ is the principle that a descent group is formed by people who believe they are related to each other by connections made through their mothers and fathers equally (sometimes called *cognatic descent*).

7. _____ is the principle that a descent group is formed by people who believe they are related to each other by links made through either men or women.

8. A kinship group that consists of the relatives of one person or group of siblings is known as a _____.

9. A _____ is a social group formed by people connected by father-child links.

10. A _____ is a social group formed by people connected by mother-child links.

11. _____ are composed of the consanguineal members of descent groups who believe they can trace their descent from known ancestors.

12. A _____ is a descent group formed by members who believe they have a common (sometimes mythical) ancestor, even if they cannot specify the genealogical links.

13. A mode of hierarchical social organization in which groups beyond the most basic emerge only in opposition to other groups on the same hierarchical level is called _____.

14. _____ is the transfer of certain symbolically significant goods from the family of the groom to the family of the bride on the occasion of their marriage. It represents compensation to the wife's lineage for the loss of her labor and her childbearing capacities.

15. _____ is connection through marriage.

16. The criterion of _____ is employed in the analysis of kinship terminologies to indicate a distinction between kin who are believed to be in a direct line and those who are "off to one side," linked to the speaker by a lineal relative.

17. The criterion of _____ is employed in the analysis of kinship terminologies to indicate that kinship terms referring to the mother's side of the family are distinguished from those referring to the father's side of the family.

18. _____ are the children of a person's parents' same-sex siblings (a father's brother's children or a mother's sister's children).

19. _____ are the children of a person's parents' opposite-sex siblings (a father's sister's children or a mother's brother's children).

20. _____ is the practice in which a line that receives a wife from a certain different line in one generation provides one back to the next generation (sometimes called *father's sister's daughter marriage*).

21. _____ is the practice in which a line always gets wives from the same line and gives wives to a different line (sometimes called *mother's brother's daughter marriage*).

22. Ritual coparenthood in Latin America and Spain, established through the Roman Catholic practice of having godparents for children, is known as _____.

23. Kinship connections based on descent are called _____ connections.

Multiple Choice Questions

1. To say that kinship is an idiom means that kinship is _____.
   a. a way of thinking and speaking about the social world
   b. the same as biology
   c. not important in social life
   d. both a and b

2. Kinship principles serve to _____.
   a. define social groups
   b. locate people within groups
   c. position people and groups in relation to one another in time and space
   d. all of the above

3. Sex:Gender::
   a. Biology:Culture
   b. Male:Female
   c. Behavior:Belief
   d. Kinship:Marriage

4. The study of kinship became important in anthropology because _____.
    a. kinship could be reduced to biology, and thus could make cross-cultural comparison objective
    b. it showed how people could maintain social order without the institution of the state
    c. it enabled anthropologists to explain why some societies had remained primitive and others had advanced
    d. kinship no longer existed in Western societies

5. The kinship strategy that is based on the assumption that the most significant kin relationships must be traced through the mother or the father only is called _____.
    a. bilateral descent
    b. matrilineal descent
    c. patrilineal descent
    d. unilineal descent

6. The most important feature of lineages is that they are _____.
    a. alliances
    b. corporate
    c. equal
    d. part of clans

7. The "patrilineal puzzle" refers to the fact that _____.
    a. people trace their descent from only one side of the family
    b. inheritances get passed from generation to generation
    c. women who are not part of the lineage produce the children for the lineage
    d. men must leave their lineages to reproduce them

8. The kinship criterion that distinguishes relatives on the basis of connection through marriage is _____.
    a. affinity
    b. bifurcation
    c. collaterality
    d. generation

9. In the Iroquois system, _____.
    a. parallel cousins are merged with siblings
    b. cross cousins and parallel cousins are merged with siblings
    c. cross cousins are merged with all patrilineal relatives
    d. parallel cousins are called by the same term used for cross cousins

10. In the late 20th century European society, the term "natural parent" has come to mean _____.
    a. someone who does not take on the social role of parent
    b. someone to whom special reproductive techniques are applied
    c. someone who combines both the biological and legal attributes of parenthood
    d. someone who is not biologically responsible for the children he or she rears

Arguing Anthropology

Questions for discussion and thought:

1. How does adoption fit into the American theory of kinship? Are adoptive parents "really" parents, or are they something else?

2. In what ways might "blended families," single-parent families by choice, or nonreproductive sexual relationships affect kinship patterns in a given society?

ANSWER KEY

Key Terms Review

1. Kinship
2. Marriage
3. descent
4. sex
5. gender
6. Bilateral descent
7. Unilineal descent
8. bilateral kindred
9. patrilineage
10. matrilineage
11. Lineages
12. clan
13. segmentary opposition
14. Bridewealth
15. Affinity
16. collaterality
17. bifurcation
18. Parallel cousins
19. Cross cousins
20. Direct exchange marriage
21. asymmetrical exchange marriage
22. *compadrazgo*
23. consanguineal

Multiple Choice Questions

1. a
2. d
3. a
4. b
5. d
6. b
7. c
8. a
9. a
10. c

Chapter 19: Marriage and the Family

STUDY STRATEGY: WRITING ESSAY ANSWERS II

Let's discuss another essay question and answer. This one comes from a set of questions which had been distributed one week in advance of a test. The instructor chose two of the questions for the exam. The students had a chance to prepare for the exam, but did not know which questions they would actually have to answer until they walked into the room to take the exam. (The answers included here are based on actual student answers that have been edited for this Study Guide.)

Question

What is marriage, from an anthropological perspective? Describe some of the variations on marriage which ethnographers have discovered in different societies. For each form of marriage you describe, explain how that form of marriage deals with the sexuality and reproductive capacity of the married partners. What makes polyandry significant in this regard?

Mental Conversation

Carrying on a conversation with yourself mentally as you analyze the question can be a helpful way to count the separate parts of the question and to decide what information to include in your answer for each part. After reading this question on marriage, a student might have the following mental conversation with himself/herself:
"Okay, this question contains several parts:

1. What is marriage, from an anthropological perspective? I'll have to give a definition. What information should I include in my definition?
2. Describe some of the variations on marriage which ethnographers have discovered in different societies. The question stated some of the variations—not all variations. I'll have to define each type of marriage. And I should give examples for each variation from different societies. What examples did we discuss in class? What examples were in the textbook?
3. For each form of marriage you describe, explain how that form of marriage deals with the sexuality and reproductive capacity of the married partners. Okay, when I tell about each form, I'll also have to include information on how that society works out sexual exclusivity and reproductive rights.
4. What makes polyandry significant in this regard? I'll definitely have to include polyandry as a form of marriage and tell how it is different in the sexuality and reproductive capacity aspect."

Writing the Answer

When writing an essay answer, consider both content and structure. After thinking about the content of your answer, decide upon the structure. Divide the answer into an introduction, body, and summary or conclusion. If the question contains many parts, as the one above does, you may want to restate and answer the first part in the first paragraph (in this case the answer includes information on the definition of marriage). Second, restate and answer the next part of the question (in this case the answer includes information on the forms of marriage and sexual and reproductive capacity). The summary briefly restates the main points.

Example of Answer Receiving Full Credit

Although answers that receive full credit vary, each of them will include a wealth of information written in an organized, easy to follow manner. The following answer is representative of the answers that received full credit on the test. In paragraph one, the introduction, the student rephrased part of the question, "From an anthropological perspective . . . ," and gave the definition of marriage. Paragraphs two through six include information on various forms of marriage, the societies containing these forms, and the sexual and reproductive capacity of the married partners. Paragraph seven sums up some main points.

From an anthropological perspective, each culture has its own definition of marriage. However, a general definition of marriage includes four conditions: (1) A woman and a man are involved; (2) each partner has the right to sexual relations; (3) the children will be considered legitimate; and (4) the relatives of both husband and wife are connected because of the the union.

I will discuss two forms of marriage: monogamy and polygamy. For the most part, monogamy is practiced in the Western world. In this form of marriage there is one wife and one husband, and the children born to this union are legitimate. The husband and wife have full rights to sexual relations with each other. However, in some countries the men may also have sexual relationships outside the marriage. Therefore, it is recognized that men have a separate sexual and reproductive capacity. This is not true for women.

Serial monogamy, another variation of monogamy is practiced in the United States and other highly industrialized nations. The divorce rate is high in the United States, and people remarry. So you have serial marriages, one marriage after the other. In each marriage there is still one husband and wife, and the children from the union are considered legitimate.

Polygamy can be divided into two subcategories: polygyny and polyandry. Polygyny is a form of marriage which allows a man to have multiple wives. For example, Islamic societies allow men to have four wives if the man can support his wives and children. It is accepted that the men (not women) in this form of marriage also have separate sexual and reproductive capacity. One disadvantage to this form of marriage is that there may be a woman shortage if men take multiple wives.

Polyandry, another subcategory of polygamy, is a form of marriage in which a wife may take multiple husbands. For example, in Tibet a wife may marry brothers; this is termed "fraternal polyandry." All the brothers have equal sexual rights with the wife, and all their children are considered legitimate. In some situations all the brothers act as "father" to the children; in other situations one brother acts as "father."

In addition to fraternal polyandry, there is associated polyandry. In this form of marriage a wife may marry multiple men who are unrelated. Again, all the men are considered fathers to the children. In both fraternal and associated polyandry, women have separate sexual and reproductive capacity.

To summarize, monogamy and polygamy are two forms of marriage, with polygamy divided into polygyny and polyandry. Polyandry is subdivided into fraternal and associated polyandry. Except in polyandry, men have the greatest sexual freedom. Children in all forms of marriage are considered legitimate.

Other Answers

Answers which received "B" grades were very good, but they lacked some information. For example, the student might not have given the countries/regions where the particular form of marriage was practiced, or not have included the full definition of marriage. These answers were, however, generally organized so that the instructor could follow the line of thought.

Answers from which quite a few points were deducted lacked both content and structure. Some students confused the forms of marriages and gave the wrong definitions and examples for the forms. Other answers totally lacked structure: instead of categorizing the information for each form of marriage into a paragraph, the student just wrote whatever came to mind. Consider the following example (notice the annotations):

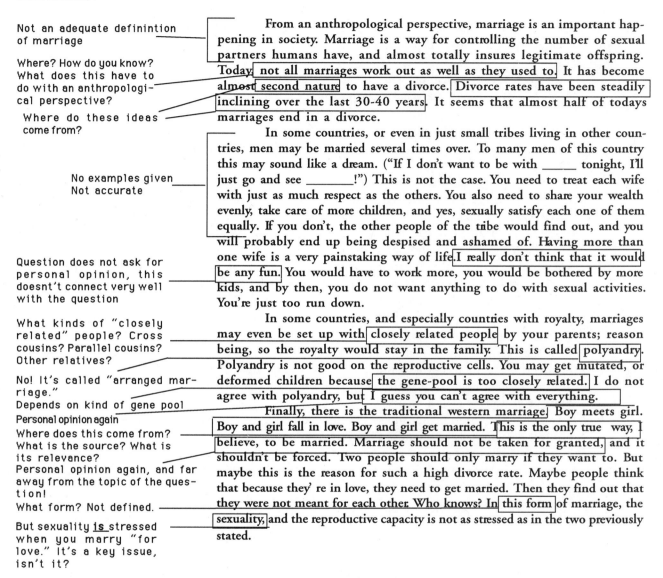

Not an adequate definintion of marriage

Where? How do you know? What does this have to do with an anthropological perspective?

Where do these ideas come from?

No examples given
Not accurate

Question does not ask for personal opinion, this doesn't connect very well with the question

What kinds of "closely related" people? Cross cousins? Parallel cousins? Other relatives?

No! It's called "arranged marriage."
Depends on kind of gene pool
Personal opinion again
Where does this come from? What is the source? What is its relevance?
Personal opinion again, and far away from the topic of the question!
What form? Not defined.

But sexuality **is** stressed when you marry "for love." It's a key issue, isn't it?

From an anthropological perspective, marriage is an important happening in society. Marriage is a way for controlling the number of sexual partners humans have, and almost totally insures legitimate offspring. Today not all marriages work out as well as they used to. It has become almost second nature to have a divorce. Divorce rates have been steadily inclining over the last 30-40 years. It seems that almost half of todays marriages end in a divorce.

In some countries, or even in just small tribes living in other countries, men may be married several times over. To many men of this country this may sound like a dream. ("If I don't want to be with _____ tonight, I'll just go and see _____!") This is not the case. You need to treat each wife with just as much respect as the others. You also need to share your wealth evenly, take care of more children, and yes, sexually satisfy each one of them equally. If you don't, the other people of the tribe would find out, and you will probably end up being despised and ashamed of. Having more than one wife is a very painstaking way of life. I really don't think that it would be any fun. You would have to work more, you would be bothered by more kids, and by then, you do not want anything to do with sexual activities. You're just too run down.

In some countries, and especially countries with royalty, marriages may even be set up with closely related people by your parents; reason being, so the royalty would stay in the family. This is called polyandry. Polyandry is not good on the reproductive cells. You may get mutated, or deformed children because the gene-pool is too closely related. I do not agree with polyandry, but I guess you can't agree with everything. Finally, there is the traditional western marriage. Boy meets girl. Boy and girl fall in love. Boy and girl get married. This is the only true way, I believe, to be married. Marriage should not be taken for granted, and it shouldn't be forced. Two people should only marry if they want to. But maybe this is the reason for such a high divorce rate. Maybe people think that because they're in love, they need to get married. Then they find out that they were not meant for each other. Who knows? In this form of marriage, the sexuality, and the reproductive capacity is not as stressed as in the two previously stated.

Overall, this answer is vague and superficial. The student did not define the terms as requested, nor give concrete examples.

Summary

Students who receive dismal grades often know the information; however, their writing style lacks clarity. If you believe you know the information but do not know how to organize your ideas, seek writing help from a tutor. English departments often have a Writing Center to help students. Your anthropology department may also have a tutor who can help you with content and structure. If you are studying, you want your grade to reflect your efforts.

EXERCISES

Key Terms Review

Use the appropriate key term(s) in each sentence that follows.

affinal
avunculocal
bridewealth
consanguineal
endogamy
exogamy

extended family
joint family
marriage
matrilocal
monogamy
neolocal

nuclear family
patrilocal
polyandry
polygamy
polygyny

1. _____ is an institution that prototypically involves a man and a woman, transforms the status of the participants, carries implications about permitted sexual access, gives the offspring a position in the society, and establishes connections between the kin of the husband and the kin of the wife.

2. Kinship connections established through marriage are called _____ connections.

3. Kinship connections based on descent are called _____ connections.

4. _____ is marriage within a defined social group.

5. Marriage outside a defined social group is known as _____.

6. _____ residence is a postmarital residence pattern in which a married couple sets up an independent household at a place of the couple's own choosing.

7. _____ residence is a postmarital residence pattern in which a married couple lives with (or near) the husband's father.

8. _____ residence is a postmarital residence pattern in which a married couple lives with (or near) the wife's mother.

9. _____ residence is a postmarital residence pattern in which a married couple lives with (or near) the husband's mother's brother (from *avuncular*, "of uncles").

10. The marriage pattern in which a person may be married to only one spouse at a time is called _____.

11. The marriage pattern in which a person may be married to more than one spouse at a time is called _____.

12. The marriage pattern in which a man may be married to more than one wife simultaneously is called _____.

13. _____ is a marriage pattern in which a woman may be married to more than one husband simultaneously.

14. _____ is the transfer of certain symbolically significant goods from the family of the groom to the family of the bride on the occasion of their marriage. It represents compensation to the wife's lineage for the loss of her labor and her childbearing capacities.

15. A(n) _____ is a family pattern made up of two generations: the parents and their unmarried children.

16. A(n) _____ is a family pattern made up of three generations living together: parents, married children, and grandchildren.

17. A(n) _____ is a family pattern made up of brothers and their wives or sisters and their husbands (along with their children) living together.

Multiple Choice Questions

1. Which of the following may be considered a prototypical criterion of marriage?
   a. it involves a man and a woman
   b. it stipulates the degree of sexual access allowed the partners
   c. it creates ties between the kin of the bride and the kin of the groom
   d. all of the above

2. When a woman marries another woman among the Nuer, _____.
   a. the female husband takes on the social role of a man
   b. they take turns herding the cattle
   c. children born to the wife belong to the female husband's lineage
   d. both a and c

3. Marriage outside a specific group is called _____.
   a. endogamy
   b. exogamy
   c. polyandry
   d. polygyny

4. Which two marriage patterns are similar to each other regarding the control of female sexuality?
   a. monogamy and polygyny
   b. monogamy and polyandry
   c. polygyny and polyandry
   d. monogamy and polygamy

5. Polyandry is found in which of the following regions of the world?
   a. Tibet and Nepal
   b. South India and Sri Lanka
   c. Northern Nigeria and Northern Cameroon
   d. all of the above

6. When anthropologists say that marriage is transaction, they mean that _____.
   a. in a matrilineal society, the wife's family pays for her husband
   b. it takes a long time for a marriage to take effect
   c. there is a flow of rights and obligations involving both sides
   d. bridewealth or a dowry is paid

7. Polygynous households differ from nuclear families in their internal dynamics along the following dimension(s): _____.
   a. relationships of husband and wife/wives
   b. relationships among children
   c. relationships of children and parents
   d. all of the above

8. Families in which several generations live together in a single household are called _____.
   a. nuclear families
   b. extended families
   c. joint families
   d. traditional families

9. In the case of Los Pinos, in the Dominican Republic, when a migration cycle started, separation was usually between _____.
   a. spouses, and was permanent
   b. spouses, and was temporary
   c. parents and children, and was permanent
   d. parents and children, and was temporary

10. Although lesbian couples in Mombasa may violate the prototype for sexual relations, they do not violate _____.
    a. relations of rank
    b. traditional law
    c. kinship relations
    d. the requirement to be married

Arguing Anthropology

Questions for discussion and thought:

1. Marriages in a number of places in the world today continue to be arranged, sometimes by families, sometimes by professional matchmakers. Many people raised in western European or North American contexts find this hard to imagine. What are the advantages of arranged marriages?

2. Sometimes, early in a marriage, a North American spouse may blurt out, "Who did I marry, anyway, you or your family?" What could lead someone to such a remark, and how could it be considered naive?

ANSWER KEY

Key Terms Review

1. Marriage
2. affinal
3. consanguineal
4. Endogamy
5. exogamy
6. Neolocal
7. Patrilocal
8. Matrilocal
9. Avunculocal
10. monogamy
11. polygamy
12. polygyny
13. Polyandry
14. Bridewealth
15. nuclear family
16. extended family
17. joint family

Multiple Choice Questions

1. d
2. d
3. b
4. a
5. d
6. c
7. d
8. b
9. b
10. a

Chapter 20: Beyond Kinship

STUDY STRATEGY: USING THE STRATEGIES OF CHARTING AND MAPPING TO ORGANIZE INFORMATION

This chapter, Beyond Kinship, discusses how and why people who are nonkin interact in their daily lives. You can use charting and mapping to organize ideas for several sections of this chapter.

Charting Ideas to Enhance Comprehension and Recall of Information

The first major section of this chapter, Kin-Based Versus Nonkin-Based Societies, is divided into three parts: (1) Status Versus Contract Relationships, (2) Mechanical Versus Organic Solidarity, and (3) Ascribed Status and Achieved Status. The ideas in parts 1, 2, and 3 are compared and contrasted. When writers compare and contrast ideas, the information can usually be organized into charts. Complete the following charts as you read and study this section.

Status Versus Contract Relationships		
Type	How is Society Organized (Relationship between People?)	Example
Status		
Contract		

Mechanical Versus Organic Solidarity			
Type of Solidarity	Explain how the relationship is organized	Advantages? Disadvantages?	Example
Mechanical			
Organic			

Ascribed Versus Achieved Status		
Type of Solidarity	Definition/Explanation	Example
Ascribed		
Achieved		

Mapping Ideas to Enhance Comprehension and Recall of Information

When mapping information, you use a diagram to show the relationship, the connection, between ideas. Let's map the next major section of this chapter, Metaphorical Kin Revisited. The main heading appears on top, and the subheadings underneath. Take notes on the information for each subheading. After completing this map, map the rest of the sections in this chapter.

```
                    ┌─────────────────────────────┐
                    │  Metaphorical Kin Revisited  │
                    └─────────────────────────────┘
         ┌────────────────────┘            └────────────────────────────────┐
┌──────────────────┐                    ┌─────────────────────────────────────────┐
│    Friendship    │                    │ The Kinship in Non-Kin Relationships    │
└──────────────────┘                    └─────────────────────────────────────────┘
```

*Define term: *Explain and give examples of
institutionalized friendship   kinship between nonkin for
                                         different societies

*How are friends like kin?
Not like kin? Examples?

To summarize, chapters 1 and 11 were outlined using the main headings and subheadings. The headings were turned into questions, and you took notes on the information. Mapping is like outlining, except it is done using a diagram. Some students like to outline, while some students like to map because they can visualize the information in their map. If information can be categorized, charting is an effective method. You have to decide what study strategies you like and what strategies fit the information you have to learn.

EXERCISES

Key Terms Review

Use the appropriate key term(s) in each sentence that follows.

achieved statuses
age sets   egalitarian societies   secret society
ascribed statuses   ethnicity   sodalities
caste   mechanical solidarity   status
class   organic solidarity   stratified societies
clientage   race
division of labor   role

1. A _____ is a particular social position in a group.

2. The rights and duties associated with a status form a _____.

3. _____ is the sense of fellow-feeling and interdependence in so-called "primitive"

   societies, based on such similarities as language and mode of livelihood.

4. _____ is the sense of fellow-feeling and interdependence in so-called "modern" societies, based on specializations of different social groups; like the organs in a body, each group is necessary for the survival of the society.

5. The _____ is work specialization within a society.

6. Social positions assigned at birth are _____.

7. Social positions attained by individual performance are _____.

8. _____ are nonkin forms of social organization: special-purpose groupings that may be organized on the basis of age, sex, economic role, and personal interest.

9. _____ are nonkin forms of social organization that are composed of men born within a specified time span and are part of a sequence that proceeds through maturity and old age.

10. Nonkin forms of social organization that initiate young men or women into social adulthood and control certain knowledge that is known only to initiated members are called _____ .

11. Societies with no great differences in wealth, power, or prestige dividing members from one another are called _____.

12. Societies in which there is a permanent hierarchy that accords some members privileged access to wealth, power, and prestige are called _____.

13. A _____ is a ranked group within a hierarchically stratified society that is closed and prohibits individuals to move from one group to another.

14. A _____ is a ranked group within a hierarchically stratified society that is open and allows individuals to move upward or downward from one group to another.

15. A social grouping based on perceived physical differences and cloaked in the language of biology is called a _____.

16. _____ is a set of prototypically descent-based cultural criteria that people in a group are believed to share.

17. The institution linking individuals from upper and lower levels in a stratified society is called _____.

Multiple Choice Questions

1. Status:Role::
   a. Position:Performance
   b. Ascribed:Achieved
   c. Mechanical:Organic
   d. Society:Culture

2. The status of Prime Minister of Canada is _____.
   a. achieved
   b. ascribed
   c. metaphorical
   d. kin-based

3. For the Bangwa of Cameroon, the prototypes of best friends are _____.
   a. brothers-in-law
   b. joking relatives
   c. sister and brother
   d. twins

4. Which institution promotes the feeling of diffuse and enduring solidarity in its members?
   a. friendship
   b. kinship
   c. sodalities
   d. all of the above

5. Age sets are _____.
   a. kinship systems made of people in five generations
   b. patterns of social interaction in which people of the same age prefer to spend time together
   c. a sequence of units composed of men of about the same age
   d. fathers and sons connected to each other by ties of kinship and social responsibility

6. What is the secret in a secret society?
   a. who the members are
   b. where the meetings are held
   c. the knowledge held by members
   d. why people join

7. According to Karl Marx, class membership in capitalist society is determined by _____.
   a. people's relationship to the means of production
   b. hard work and good luck
   c. an accident of birth
   d. occupational specialization

8. Jatis in Gopalpur are distinguished by _____.
   a. what members eat
   b. the members' traditional occupations
   c. the members' physical capacities
   d. both a and b

9. Which of the following were NOT recognized as castas in seventeenth century Mexico?
    a. *castizo*
    b. *criollo*
    c. *morocho*
    d. *mulato*

10. Nonkin social ties provide ways for people to _____.
    a. link themselves across kinship boundaries
    b. reinforce lineage boundaries
    c. direct their attention to broader social concerns
    d. both a and c

Arguing Anthropology

Questions for discussion and thought:

1. Why are nonkin social ties so important in places like the United States and Canada today?

2. Why is being "friendly" so important in student culture?

ANSWER KEY

Key Terms Review

1. status
2. role
3. Mechanical solidarity
4. Organic solidarity
5. division of labor
6. ascribed statuses
7. achieved statuses
8. Sodalities
9. Age sets
10. secret societies
11. egalitarian societies
12. stratified societies
13. caste
14. class
15. race
16. Ethnicity
17. clientage

Multiple Choice Questions

1. a
2. b
3. d
4. d
5. c
6. c
7. a
8. d
9. c
10. d

Chapter 21: Social Organization and Power

STUDY STRATEGY: **USING THE SUMMARIES AS STUDY GUIDES**

A previous chapter noted that constructing your own list of questions from each numbered point in the summary was an effective study strategy. Answering your questions provides you with feedback as to whether or not you have a grasp of the main concepts and some important details.

Consider the following questions for this chapter. In addition, what other questions could you ask about information in your lecture notes?

1. Define social organization. Why should we investigate the power people have to reproduce or change their social organizations?
2. Each of the following groups tried to explain cross-cultural similarities and differences in social organizations: anthropologists, evolutionists, environmental determinists, and biological determinists. How did each explain them?
3. How does power operate in Western and non-Western societies?
4. How does Western and non-Western thought differ concerning the necessity of having a state as a governing force?
5. Why do we obey institutionalized power?
6. Discuss power as control. What is the effect of the perspective which considers power as control?
7. How is power viewed in stateless societies? Why?
8. Why is our power to interpret our experiences in the manner in which we wish important?
9. How may rulers view power? How can a ruler's power be undermined?
10. How and why does political power affect our lives? How may oppressed peoples resist the power exerted by their rulers?
11. Are debates always negotiated to the satisfaction of all groups? Why or why not? What is the effect of having to agree to something you oppose?
12. What does the phrase, "bargaining for reality" mean? What occurs when we bargain? Why is the past used as a lesson for the present or future?

If you are tired and experiencing problems concentrating while studying, write out the answers. Reciting and writing out the answers are active methods of studying, and will help you to learn and recall the information during your test.

EXERCISES

Key Terms Review

Use the appropriate key term(s) in each sentence that follows.

alienation	consensus	persuasion
anomie	essentially negotiable concepts	political anthropology
autonomy	legitimacy	power
coercion	negotiation	social organization

1. The patterning of human interdependence in a given society through the actions and decisions of its members is that society's _____.

2. _____ is transformative capacity: the ability to transform a given situation.

3. The study of social power in human society is the subject of _____.

4. Power based on physical force is called _____.

5. Power based on group consensus is called _____.

6. _____ is defined as the right not be forced against one's will to conform to someone else's wishes.

7. _____ is an agreement to which all parties collectively give their assent.

8. Power based on verbal argument is called _____.

9. _____ is a pervasive sense of rootlessness and normlessness in a society.

10. _____ is the term used by Karl Marx to describe the deep separation that workers seemed to experience between their innermost sense of identity and the labor they were forced to perform in order to earn enough money to live.

11. Reaching a settlement or agreement by means of verbal discussion is called

    _____.

12. Culturally recognized concepts that evoke a wide range of meanings and whose relevance in any particular context must be negotiated are called _____.

Multiple Choice Questions

1. Social organization refers to _____.
    a. a set of ideas people have about the people with whom they should have collective relations
    b. the beliefs and practices in a given society, associated with marriage, kinship, and friendship
    c. the patterning of human interdependence in a given society
    d. all of the above

2. Which single explanation of the laws of social organization do anthropologists prefer?
    a. historical
    b. environmental
    c. biological
    d. none of the above

3. Eric Wolf describes three modes of social power. Which of the following is NOT one of them?
    a. interpersonal power
    b. individual power
    c. organizational power
    d. structural power

4. A group of students get together to select someone to present their complaints about a course to the dean. They agree that the representative selected will be able to negotiate directly with the dean without having to get their approval for every decision. What the group has granted its representative is an example of power as _____.
   a. alienation
   b. coercion
   c. anomie
   d. legitimacy

5. Which of the following views of power is traditional in Western state societies?
   a. power as coercion
   b. power as an independent entity
   c. power as a way of investing the world with meaning
   d. power as a panhuman force

6. When coercion no longer works, what remains is a confrontation between alternative accounts of experience. Which is the best term to describe how one account comes to dominate?
   a. consensus
   b. force
   c. persuasion
   d. all of the above

7. According to James Scott, foot-dragging, desertion, pilfering, slander, arson, and sabotage are examples of _____.
   a. everyday forms of peasant resistance
   b. routine repression
   c. unusual forms of peasant resistance
   d. unusual forms of repression

8. Before the Bolivian tin mines were nationalized, the ch'alla ritual embodied _____.
   a. conflict between mine owners and mine workers
   b. harmonious ties between mine owners and mine workers
   c. conflict between male miners and female miners
   d. cooperation between male miners and female miners

9. What makes a concept "essentially negotiable"?
   a. There is an element of uncertainty built into the term so that people can argue about using it.
   b. It is controlled by the upper class.
   c. It needs someone of real authority and power to decide what the term means in a certain situation and then to apply it.
   d. It is a term introduced from another culture and is therefore difficult to define.

10. What do the *rondas campesinas* of northern Peru have in common with the Peruvian government's justice system?
    a. They both claim to uphold the law and the constitution.
    b. They both rely on a system of judges.
    c. They both require some kind of payoff to guarantee a successful outcome.
    d. nothing

Arguing Anthropology

Questions for discussion and thought:

1. When students feel powerless in a university environment, do they employ strategies similar to the ones discussed in the sections The Power of the Weak and Negotiation in the text?

2. How will nations decide to support one faction rather than another in international trouble spots, when the old lessons of history that saw the world in terms of superpower rivalry no longer seem to apply?

ANSWER KEY

Key Terms Review

1. social organization
2. Power
3. political anthropology
4. coercion
5. legitimacy
6. Autonomy
7. Consensus
8. persuasion
9. Anomie
10. Alienation
11. negotiation
12. essentially negotiable concepts

Multiple Choice Questions

1. d
2. d
3. b
4. d
5. a
6. c
7. a
8. b
9. a
10. a

Chapter 22: Making a Living

STUDY STRATEGY: FINAL EVALUATION OF STUDY STRATEGIES

Since you are at the end of this textbook, this is an appropriate time for you to stop and evaluate how you are doing in this anthropology course. In addition, you should plan what you will do for the rest of the course and your final test.

At the Chapter 12 midpoint evaluation, you answered the following questions. Answer these questions again.

Final Evaluation	
1. What is your grade now? What grade do you want?	
2. What do you still have to do? • *Textbook:* How much do you have to read for the next test? • *Lecture notes:* Do you have a good set of notes? Missing notes? Vague notes? • *Papers/Projects:* What do you have to do?	
3. What type of test will you have? • *Multiple choice?* Fact questions? Application questions? • *Essay test?*	
4. How much background knowledge do you have of information in the rest of this book?	
5. What strategies are effective for you? • *Reading your textbook:* Using the Preview/Read/Review method? Asking numerous questions to test your knowledge? • *Note-taking:* Cross-checking your notes with classmates? Reviewing & reciting often?	

• *Charting & mapping:* Would organizing information into a chart or map help? • *Notecards:* Would writing vocabulary cards help? • *Group study:* Have a friend or friends to study with? • *Instructor and tutors:* Getting extra help with your questions? • *Tests:* Predicting test questions? If you have an essay test, are you writing out answers to practice and determine if you know the information? • *Procrastination:* Are you avoiding the procrastination virus? Allowing adequate time to read and learn the information?	
6. What additional strategies would help you?	
7. What is your attitude? Positive? Negative? Overwhelmed? How can you make life more comfortable for yourself?	
8. What can you do to motivate yourself to study?	

In short, analyze what you must do, decide upon the study strategies that will work for you, monitor your comprehension and retention and modify or adjust your strategies for your final test. Now, what is your plan for the rest of this anthropology course?

EXERCISES

Key Terms Review

Use the appropriate key term(s) in each sentence that follows.

affluence
consumption
distribution
ecology
economy
ecozone
exchange
extensive agriculture
food collectors
food producers

formalists
ideology
intensive agriculture
labor
market exchange
means of production
mechanized industrial agricul-
    ture
mode of production
modes of exchange

neoclassical economic theory
niche
production
rational
reciprocity
redistribution
relations of production
scarcity
subsistence strategies
substantivists

1. The assumption that resources (for example, money) will never be plentiful enough for people to obtain all the goods they desire is called _____.

2. The _____ comprises the material life process of society.

3. The patterns of production, distribution, and consumption that members of a society employ to ensure the satisfaction of the basic material survival needs of human beings are called _____.

4. Those who gather, fish, or hunt for food are called _____.

5. _____ are those who depend on domesticated plants and/or animals for food.

6. A form of cultivation that requires moving farm plots every few years as the soil becomes exhausted, based on the technique of clearing uncultivated land, burning the brush, and planting the crops in the ash-enriched soil is called _____.

7. _____ is a form of cultivation that employs plows, draft animals, irrigation, fertilizer, etc. to bring much land under cultivation, to use it year after year, and to produce significant surpluses.

8. Large-scale farming and animal husbandry that is highly dependent on industrial methods of technology and production is called _____.

9. The transformation of nature's raw materials into a form suitable for human use is called _____.

10. The allocation of goods and services is called _____.

11. The using up of material goods necessary for human survival is called _____.

12. _____ is one form of distribution found in many societies.

13. _____ is a formal attempt to explain the workings of capitalist enterprise, with particular attention to distribution.

14. Economic anthropologists who adopted formal neoclassical economic theory to explain economic activities in non-Western societies are known as _____.

15. In Western economic terms, to be _____ means to be concerned first and foremost with one's individual self-interest as defined in terms of the market: to buy cheap, to sell dear, to realize a profit.

16. Economic anthropologists who criticized the formalists for being ethnocentric, arguing that economic institutions cannot be explained apart from the particular cultural contexts in which they are embedded, are known as _____.

17. _____ are patterns according to which distribution takes place: reciprocity, redistribution, and market exchange.

18. The exchange of goods and services of equal value is called _____. Anthropologists distinguish three forms of it: _____, in which neither the time nor the value of the return are specified; _____, in which a return of equal value is expected within a specified time limit; and _____, in which parties to the exchange expect to get the better of the exchange.

19. A mode of exchange that requires some form of centralized social organization to receive economic contributions from all members of the group and to divert them in such a way that every group member is provided for is known as _____.

20. _____ is the exchange of goods (_____) calculated in terms of a multipurpose medium of exchange and standard of value (_____) and carried on by means of a supply-demand-price mechanism (_____).

21. _____ is the activity linking human social groups to the material world around them; for Karl Marx, it is therefore always social.

22. A specific, historically occurring set of social relations through which labor is deployed to wrest energy from nature by means of tools, skills, organization, and knowledge is called a _____.

23. The _____ consist of the tools, skills, organization, and knowledge used to extract energy from nature.

24. The social relations linking the people who use a given means of production within a particular mode of production are called the _____.

25. _____ is made up of those products of consciousness—such as morality, religion, and metaphysics—that purport to explain to people who they are and to justify to them the kind of lives they lead.

26. The study of the ways in which living species relate to one another and to their natural environment is called _____.

27. A _____ is the portion of the natural world on which a species depends for the satisfaction of its material needs.

28. The particular mix of plant and animal species occupying any particular region of the earth is called a(n) _____.

29. _____ is the condition of having more than enough of whatever is required to satisfy consumption needs.

Multiple Choice Questions

1. The assumption that people's resources will never be great enough for them to obtain all the goods they desire is called _____.
   a. scarcity
   b. poverty
   c. utility
   d. affluence

2. The different ways in which people in different societies go about meeting their survival needs are called _____.
   a. industries
   b. subsistence strategies
   c. agriculture
   d. energy collecting

3. Anthropologists have generally agreed that economic activity is usefully subdivided into three phases. Which of the following is NOT one of the phases?
   a. consumption
   b. distribution
   c. production
   d. processing

4. Economic anthropologists who are influenced by marxian approaches argue that _____ cannot be understood without first studying _____.
   a. exchange; production
   b. exchange; consumption
   c. production; exchange
   d. production; consumption

5. It was _____ who argued that economic theories designed to make sense of the capitalist market and its effects were NOT well suited to non-Western, non-capitalist societies.
   a. formalists
   b. economists
   c. neoclassicists
   d. substantivists

6. A mode of production is a _____.
   a. method of industrial manufacturing
   b. set of tools, skills, organization, and knowledge that a society uses to extract energy from nature
   c. set of social relations through which labor is organized in feudal societies
   d. way to make sure that people do what is necessary in a given society

7. Which term is used to refer to the beliefs that explain and justify the relations of production?
   a. anomie
   b. ideology
   c. reciprocity
   d. ecology

8. Cultural ecology is an attempt to apply _____.
   a. marxian theory to consumption
   b. substantivist theory to consumption
   c. socioecology to people and their societies
   d. dialectical biology to human culture

9. According to Marshall Sahlins, which of the following is a route to affluence?
   a. colonial conquest
   b. producing much
   c. desiring little
   d. both b and c

10. If there were no relationship between the material and the meaningful in the consumption of food, then Americans would _____.
    a. pay more for beef tongue than for steak
    b. eat dogs and horses as well as cattle and pigs
    c. pay little attention to what they ate
    d. all of the above

Arguing Anthropology

Questions for discussion and thought:

1. From an anthropological perspective, why don't North Americans eat dogs?

2. In light of the discussion in this chapter, what might the famous phrase "You are what you eat" mean?

ANSWER KEY

Key Terms Review

1. scarcity
2. economy
3. subsistence strategies
4. food collectors
5. Food producers
6. extensive agriculture
7. Intensive agriculture
8. mechanized industrial agriculture
9. production
10. distribution
11. consumption
12. Exchange
13. Neoclassical economic theory
14. formalists
15. rational
16. substantivists
17. Modes of exchange
18. reciprocity; generalized; balanced; negative
19. redistribution
20. Market exchange; trade; money; the market
21. Labor
22. mode of production
23. means of production
24. relations of production
25. ideology
26. ecology
27. niche
28. ecozone
29. Affluence

Multiple Choice Questions

1. a
2. b
3. d
4. a
5. d
6. b
7. b
8. c
9. d
10. d

Chapter 23: The World System

EXERCISES

Key Terms Review

Use the appropriate key term(s) in each sentence that follows.

articulating modes of production
capitalism
colonialism
core
dependency theory
development-of-under
    development thesis

land tenure
modernization theory
neocolonialism
neomarxian theory
periphery
political economy

sacred persuasion
secular persuasion
use rights
world-system theory

1. _____ may be defined as cultural domination with enforced social change.

2. _____ may be understood as either (1) an economic system dominated by the supply-demand-price mechanism called *the market*; or (2) an entire way of life that grew in response to and in service of that market.

3. _____ is a holistic term that encompasses the centrality of material interest and the use of power to protect and enhance that interest.

4. Rights to use, but not own, land for farming or grazing are known as _____.

5. Land ownership is also called _____.

6. The persistence of profound social and economic entanglements linking former colonial territories to their former colonial rulers despite recovered political sovereignty is called _____.

7. _____ argues that the social change occurring in non-Western societies under colonial rule was a necessary and inevitable prelude to the higher levels of social development that had been reached by Europe and North America.

8. _____ argues that the success of "independent" capitalist nations has required the failure of "dependent" colonies or nations whose economies have been distorted to serve the needs of the dominant capitalist outsiders.

9. The _____ argues that capitalism deliberately creates "underdevelopment" in formerly prosperous areas that come under its domination.

10. _____ argues that from the late fifteenth and early sixteenth centuries European capitalism began to incorporate other regions and peoples into a system whose parts were linked together economically but not politically.

11. In world-system theory, the _____ refers to nations specializing in banking, finance, and highly skilled industrial production.

12. In world-system theory, the _____ refers to those exploited former colonies that supply colonial powers with cheap food and raw materials.

13. _____ is a political economic theory based on the work of a new generation of scholars who, though inspired by the work of Karl Marx, reinterpret or reject certain aspects of his theory when necessary.

14. _____ is an aspect of neomarxian thought that describes the links between capitalist and non-capitalist modes of production in the Third World.

15. The attempt by Western religious missionaries to pressure non-Western societies to change is called

_____.

16. The attempt by Western secular authorities to pressure non-Western societies to change is called

_____.

Multiple Choice Questions

1. Creating a reserve for the Kréen-Akaróre had what effect?
   a. The Kréen-Akaróre abandoned their gardens and aborted their babies.
   b. Their population increased and, eventually, they required more land.
   c. They became employed by establishments along the new highway.
   d. Many of them became eloquent spokespeople for environmental and other advocacy groups whose goal was protection of the Amazon Rain Forest.

2. According to the text, one significant transformation that resulted from the contact of European nations with the non-Western world was _____.
   a. the growth of cities
   b. the rise of clothing styles in Europe derived from clothing common in the colonies
   c. the development of European-style businesses under native control in the small towns in the colony
   d. the growth of an indigenous middle class

3. Which of the following is NOT a link created by the colonial political economy?
   a. different conquered communities linked within a conquered territory
   b. different conquered territories linked with one another
   c. all conquered territories linked with the country of the colonizer
   d. different colonizing countries linked with one another

4. Before the imposition of capitalism on non-Western societies, land was usually _____.
   a. subject to sale by the leader of the group
   b. held by the social group that made use of it
   c. available to anyone who wanted to use it
   d. held by people of high status who would let people of lower status work for them

5. As a result of the growth of capitalist manufacturing in the late eighteenth century, when European merchants viewed Africa, they saw a _____.
   a. need for increasing numbers of slaves
   b. need for an educated African workforce
   c. source of cheap raw materials
   d. manufacturing site with low labor costs

6. When Ivory Coast became a colony of France, the traditional order of the Baule was upset because _____.
   a. factory-spun thread was sold for cash
   b. men were made responsible for paying their wives' taxes in cash
   c. men were taught how to grow cash-crop cotton
   d. all of the above

7. The theory that agues that dependent colonies or nations must endure the reshaping of their economic structures to meet demands generated outside their borders is called _____.
   a. modernization theory
   b. dependency theory
   c. world-system theory
   d. neomarxian theory

8. New social movements may be understood as _____.
   a. revolutionary attempts to overthrow the power structure
   b. the attempt by post-Cold War governments to rally their citizens to collective action
   c. cultural institutions people construct to meet their needs, bypassing national governments
   d. an attempt to reestablish a way of life that resembles the pre-colonial culture

9. One consequence of missionary activity among the Kaguru was _____.
   a. martyrdom of scores of missionaries and their families
   b. that the Kaguru began to read the Bible and to identify themselves with the oppressed
   c. an increase in the number of Kaguru who took government jobs
   d. the rise of an indigenous African clergy

10. According to Eric Wolf, the six major peasant wars of the twentieth century were waged in order to _____.
    a. impose capitalism on a reluctant peasantry
    b. impose communism on a reluctant peasantry
    c. defend the middle peasants' way of life against the inroads of capitalism
    d. export communism from Europe to the Third World

Arguing Anthropology

Questions for discussion and thought:

1. Why should anyone care about the world's indigenous peoples?

2. What is the justification for Christian missionary activity in the non-Christian world, from the point of view of (1) missionaries; (2) the governments of the nations in which the missionaries work; (3) local people being missionized; (4) anthropologists; (5) you yourself?

ANSWER KEY

Key Terms Review

1. Colonialism
2. Capitalism
3. Political economy
4. use rights
5. land tenure
6. neocolonialism
7. Modernization theory
8. Dependency theory
9. development-of-underdevelopment thesis
10. World-system theory
11. core
12. periphery
13. Neomarxian theory
14. Articulating modes of production
15. sacred persuasion
16. secular persuasion

Multiple Choice Questions

1. a
2. a
3. d
4. b
5. c
6. d
7. b
8. c
9. b
10. c

Chapter 24: Anthropology in Everyday Life

EXERCISES

Multiple Choice Questions

1. In the late twentieth century, applied anthropology became increasingly popular and important as a result of _____.
   a. the maturation of the discipline
   b. the growing sophistication and awareness of the people with whom anthropologists have traditionally worked
   c. a growing concern about how an anthropological approach could help solve problems in the anthropologists' own societies
   d. all of the above

2. Applied anthropologists who work in international development often find themselves in programs connected with _____.
   a. agriculture
   b. industrial technology
   c. personnel work with multinational corporations
   d. all of the above

3. Why are anthropologists sometimes hesitant to make detailed policy recommendations?
   a. They are particularly aware of the problems in trying to make people, or systems, change.
   b. They have very little trust in politicians and policymakers.
   c. They are not expert in policy-making.
   d. They do not believe that people in the less-developed world should change.

4. An anthropologically oriented organization involved with human rights is _____.
   a. the American Association for the Advancement of Science
   b. the National Geographic Society
   c. Cultural Survival
   d. the Foundation for Indigenous Rights and Protections

Arguing Anthropology

Questions for discussion and thought:

1. Should anthropologists get involved in international development projects?

2. Why should people study anthropology?

ANSWER KEY

Multiple Choice Questions

1. d
2. a
3. a
4. c

References

Afflerbach, P. P. 1990. The influence of prior knowledge on expert readers' main idea construction strategies. *Reading Research Quarterly* 25 (Winter): 31-46.

Barr, R., M. L. Kamil, P. Mosenthal, P. D. Pearson, eds. 1991. *Handbook of Reading Research*: Volume 2. New York: Longman.

Bransford, J. D. 1979. *Human Cognition: Learning, Understanding and Remembering*. Belmont, CA.: Wadsworth Publishing Company.

Brown, A. and A. Palincsar. 1982. *Inducing strategic learning from texts by means of informed self-control training*. (Technical Report No. 262). Urbana, IL: Illinois University, Urbana Center for the Study of Reading. (ERIC Document Reproduction Service No. ED 220 820.)

Flippo, R. F. and D. C. Caverly, eds. 1991. *Teaching Reading and Study Strategies at The College Level*. International Reading Association, Newark, New Jersey.

Guri-Rozenblit, S. 1989. Effects of a tree diagram on students' comprehension of main ideas in a multi-thematic expository text. *Reading Research Quarterly* 24 (Spring): 236-47.

Jawitz, L. B. and P. B. 1993. Mental imagery, text illustrations, and children's story comprehension and recall. *Reading Research Quarterly* 28 (July/August): 264-73.

McCombs, F.L. and J. S. Whisler, 1989. The role of affective variables in autonomous learning. *Educational Psychologist* 24: 277-306.

Mealey, D. L. 1990. Understanding the motivation problems of at-risk college students. *Journal of Reading* 33 (May): 598-601.

Nist, S. L. and M. L. Simpson. 1989. PLAE, a validated study strategy. *Journal of Reading* 33 (December): 182-86.

Rauch, M. 1985-86. Mapping information: A useful study strategy. In *Innovative Learning Strategies*, ed. G. L. Howell, and T. J. Betenbough, 102-14. College Reading Improvement, International Reading Association.

Rauch, M. 1989-90. Charting: A study strategy. In *Innovative Learning Strategies*, ed. S. A. Biggs and T. Bullock, 67-82. College Reading Improvement, International Reading Association.

Rauch, M. 1991-92. Teaching the generation of questions-study strategy. In *Innovative Learning Strategies*, ed. T. L. Bullock and A. M. Scales, 9-16. College Reading Improvement, International Reading Association.

Sadowski, M. and A. A. Paivio. 1994. Dual coding view of imagery and verbal processes in reading comprehension. In *Theoretical Models and Processes of Reading*, ed. R. B. Ruddell, M. R. Ruddell, and H. Singer, 582-601. Newark, NJ: International Reading Association.

Stahl, N. A., J. R. King, and W. A. Henk. 1991. Enhancing students' notetaking through training and evaluation. *Journal of Reading* 34 (May): 614-22.

Wade, S. E. and R. E. Reynolds. 1989. Developing metacognitive awareness. *Journal of Reading* 33 (October): 6-14.

Weinstein, C. E., E. T. Goetz and P. A. Alexander, eds. 1988. *Learning and Study Strategies: Issues in Assessment, Instruction, and Evaluation*. New York: Academic Press, Inc.